Teach
Yourself®

Get started in Portuguese

Sue Tyson-Ward

Advisory Editor
Bruno Paul

T0271781

First published in Great Britain in 1996 by Hodder & Stoughton. An Hachette UK company.

First published in US in 1996 by The McGraw-Hill Companies, Inc.

This edition published 2014

British Library Cataloguing in Publication Data: a catalogue record for this title is available from the British Library.

ISBN 978 1444 74861

Library of Congress Catalog Card Number: on file.

10 9 8

The publisher has used its best endeavours to ensure that any website addresses referred to in this book are correct and active at the time of going to press. However, the publisher and the author have no responsibility for the websites and can make no guarantee that a site will remain live or that the content will remain relevant, decent or appropriate.

The publisher has made every effort to mark as such all words which it believes to be trademarks. The publisher should also like to make it clear that the presence of a word in the book, whether marked or unmarked, in no way affects its legal status as a trademark.

Every reasonable effort has been made by the publisher to trace the copyright holders of material in this book. Any errors or omissions should be notified in writing to the publisher, who will endeavour to rectify the situation for any reprints and future editions.

Cover image © Synthetic Alan King / Alamy

Typeset by Integra Software Services Pvt. Ltd., Pondicherry, India.

Printed and bound in Great Britain by Clays Ltd, Elcograf S.p.A.

Hodder & Stoughton policy is to use papers that are natural, renewable and recyclable products and made from wood grown in sustainable forests. The logging and manufacturing processes are expected to conform to the environmental regulations of the country of origin.

Hodder & Stoughton Ltd

338 Euston Road

London NW1 3BH

www.hodder.co.uk

Contents

Meet the author

I have had a connection with Portugal since living with a Portuguese family prior to starting my studies at Oxford in 1984. During my degree course I also spent a year in Brazil, experiences which I have drawn on frequently over the years in my teaching and writing. Since graduating with a degree in Portuguese and Spanish in 1988, I have also lived, worked and studied in Portugal, and continue to go there each year with my family, often travelling through remote regions by public transport.

I have written a number of books on Portuguese language, life and culture, as well as on living, working and buying property there. I was invited to act as language consultant for the BBC's highly-acclaimed TV series *Talk Portuguese*, and also gave initial advice for the Brazil *Inside Out* series.

I have been involved in Portuguese examinations in the UK since 1992, including roles as Moderator for GCSE speaking tests, Principal Examiner for GCSE Writing, and Principal Moderator for Asset Speaking tests; I was also the Subject Officer for Portuguese at the Awarding Body. I currently act as adviser and vetter for international examinations.

I continue to teach the language and culture in Lancaster, in North-West England, and run a Portuguese Club at my daughter's primary school. I am a keen and enthusiastic promoter of all things relating to the Portuguese-speaking world.

Sue Tyson-Ward

How this book works

Welcome to *Get Started in Portuguese*. This course is designed to increase your confidence in listening to and speaking basic Portuguese, and gives you the chance to hear many everyday situations in dialogues. It also gives you a range of insights into the way the language works, through easy-to-manage language discovery sections, and handy tips to help you get the gist of what you are learning. There are various writing, listening, and speaking exercises to guide you on your progress.

Get Started in Portuguese is the right course for you if you are a complete beginner or want to make a fresh start. It is a self-study course which will help you to understand, read and speak most of the Portuguese you will need on holiday or a business trip.

The book has two parts. The first ten units introduce you to the basic structures and grammatical points you'll need in everyday situations. Units 1–10 should be taken in order as each builds on the previous one, gradually increasing your knowledge of how Portuguese works.

Units 11 onwards deal with everyday situations such as shopping, eating, booking a room, and travelling, and give you the opportunity to put into practice the language you've acquired during the first part. These units may be taken in any order.

The recorded dialogues and audio exercises give you plenty of practice in understanding basic spoken Portuguese; they will also help you develop an authentic accent and increase your confidence in saying simple phrases. Whilst the course is predominantly European Portuguese in content, Brazilian Portuguese is also referred to, with some dialogues featuring a Brazilian speaker.

About Units 1–10

The first page of each Unit tells you what you are going to learn. There is also a cultural section introducing new topic expressions and insights into life in Portugal.

Diálogo. Each dialogue is preceded by a recording of its key new expressions for you to listen to, imitate, and learn. You are also guided in your listening by questions requiring you to focus on snippets of language as you listen. Listen to the dialogues once or twice without stopping the recording or read through them without looking anything up; try to get the gist of them. Then, using the pause button, break the dialogue into manageable chunks and try repeating each phrase out loud. This will help you acquire a more authentic accent.

The **Vocabulary lists** beneath the dialogues contain additional important words and phrases that you have heard. Try to learn them by heart. They will be practised in the rest of the unit and throughout the course.

Reading. Listen to these passages on the audio, checking you can get the gist of the passage first. Then make sure you know all the vocabulary. All key vocabulary is recorded to help you develop an authentic pronunciation.

Language discovery and **Go further**. In these sections, you may want to start by reading the example(s) then work out the grammatical point or you may prefer to read the explanation first and see how the rule applies. Once you feel confident about a particular grammar point, try to create your own examples. Discovery questions will push you in the right direction!

Practice. Each activity in this section allows you to practise one of the points introduced in the **Language discovery** sections. Some activities are audio-based. Answers to all the exercises are found in the **Key to the exercises** at the back of the book.

Língua viva. Occasional 'living language' questions based on authentic Portuguese from everyday situations, such as signs, leaflets or menus, allow you the opportunity to practise understanding the language as you might encounter it on your travels.

Test yourself. At the end of each unit you can test yourself on words and phrases you have just learnt.

Make sure you are confident with all the material in each Unit before you proceed to the next one; in this part of the book, your knowledge is being carefully constructed to enable you to start functioning in Portuguese independently.

About Units 11–17

The first page tells you what you are going to practise. You'll also find a short **Culture text** about the Unit topic and how it relates to everyday life in Portugal.

Diálogos. Each dialogue deals with a different aspect of the Unit topic. Remember to listen and pause to practise the new words and phrases out loud. Each dialogue is preceded by a recording of the key expressions, and is followed by additional useful vocabulary. You are also guided to study the dialogues carefully by means of pre-and post-listening questions.

Practice. Many of the activities are based on authentic Portuguese material. Here you can develop a feel for how things work in Portugal, as well as practise your reading skills. You will then have more confidence to cope with real situations.

The **Test yourself** section at the end of the Unit allows you to assess your progress in the situations you have been practising.

At the back of the book you will find:

The **Key to the exercises:** This contains the answers to all the exercises from the book. Some answers to the listening exercises are given on the recording itself.

Portuguese–English vocabulary: a bilingual list of all the main words from the course for easy look-up and reference.

(m) masculine

(f) feminine

(sing) singular

(pl) plural

(lit) literally

ICONS

To make your learning easier and more efficient, a system of icons indicates the actions you should take:

 Play the audio track

 Listen and pronounce

 Figure something out for yourself

 Learn key words and expressions

 Exercises coming up!

 Reading passage

 Write and make notes

 Speak Portuguese out loud (even if you're alone)

 Check your Portuguese ability (no cheating)

Learn to learn

The Discovery method

There are lots of philosophies and approaches to language learning, some practical, some quite unconventional, and far too many to list here. Perhaps you know of a few, or even have some techniques of your own. In this book we have incorporated the **Discovery method** of learning, a sort of DIY approach to language learning. What this means is that you will be encouraged throughout the course to engage your mind and figure out the language for yourself, through identifying patterns, understanding grammar concepts, noticing words that are similar to English, and more. This method promotes *language awareness*, a critical skill in acquiring a new language. As a result of your own efforts, you will be able to better retain what you have learned, use it with confidence, and, even better, apply those same skills to *continuing* to learn the language (or, indeed, another one) on your own after you've finished this book.

Everyone can succeed in learning a language – the key is to know how to learn it. Learning is more than just reading or memorizing grammar and vocabulary. It's about being an active learner, learning in real contexts, and, most importantly, *using* what you've learned in different situations. Simply put, if you **figure something out for yourself**, you're more likely to understand it. And when you use what you've learned, you're more likely to remember it.

And because many of the essential but (let's admit it!) dull details, such as grammar rules, are introduced through the **Discovery method**, you'll have more fun while learning. Soon, the language will start to make sense and you'll be relying on your own intuition to construct original sentences *independently*, not just listening and repeating.

Enjoy yourself!

Become a successful language learner

Study a little every day, between 20 and 30 minutes if possible, rather than two to three hours in one session. **Give yourself short-term goals**, e.g. work out how long you'll spend on a particular unit and work within the time limit. This will help you to **create a study habit**, much in the same way you would a sport or music. You will need to concentrate, so try to **create an environment conducive to learning** which is calm and quiet and free from distractions. As you study, do not worry about your mistakes or the things you can't remember or understand. Languages settle differently in our brains, but gradually the language will become clearer as your brain starts to make new connections. **Just give yourself enough time** and you will succeed.

2 EXPAND YOUR LANGUAGE CONTACT

As part of your study habit, try to take other opportunities to expose yourself to the language. As well as using this book you could try listening to radio and television or reading articles and blogs. Perhaps you could find information in Portuguese about a personal passion or hobby or even a news story that interests you. In time you'll find that your vocabulary and language recognition deepen and you'll become used to a range of writing and speaking styles.

3 VOCABULARY

▶ To organize your study of vocabulary, group new words under:
   a generic categories, e.g. *food, furniture*.
   b situations in which they occur, e.g. under *restaurant* you can write *waiter, table, menu, bill*.
   c functions, e.g. greetings, parting, thanks, apologizing.
▶ Say the words out loud as you read them.
▶ Write the words over and over again.
▶ Listen to the audio several times.
▶ Cover up the English side of the vocabulary list and see if you remember the meaning of the word.
▶ Associate the words with similar sounding words in English, e.g. **estudar** (*to study*) with the action of *studying*, **banco** with *bank*.
▶ Create flash cards, drawings and mind maps.

- Write words for objects around your house and stick them to objects.
- Pay attention to patterns in words, e.g. adding **bom** or **boa** to the start of a phrase often indicates a greeting, **bom dia**, **boa tarde**, **boa noite**.
- **Experiment with words.** Use the words that you learn in new contexts and find out if they are correct. For example, you learn in Unit 4 that **ter** means *to have*, e.g. **tenho dois filhos** (*I have two children / sons*), and is also used to say how old you are: **tenho 25 anos** (*I am 25 years old*). Experiment with **tenho** in new contexts, e.g. **tenho uma casa bonita** (*I have a pretty house*), **tenho um carro azul** (*I have a blue car*). Check the new phrases either in this book, a dictionary or with Portuguese speakers.

4 GRAMMAR

- To organize the study of grammar write your own grammar glossary and add new information and examples as you go along.
- **Experiment with grammar rules.** Sit back and reflect on the rules you learn. See how they compare with your own language or other languages you may already speak. Try to find out some rules on your own and be ready to spot the exceptions. By doing this you'll remember the rules better and get a feel for the language.
- Try to find examples of grammar in conversations or other articles.
- Keep a 'pattern bank' that organizes examples that can be listed under the structures you've learned.
- Use old vocabulary to practise new grammar structures.
- When you learn a new verb form, write the conjugation of several different verbs you know that follow the same form.

5 PRONUNCIATION

- When organizing the study of pronunciation keep a section of your notebook for pronunciation rules and practise those that trouble you.
- Repeat all of the conversations, line by line. Listen to yourself and try to mimic what you hear.
- Record yourself and compare yourself to a native speaker.
- Make a list of words that give you trouble and practise them.
- Study individual sounds, then full words.
- Don't forget, it's not just about pronouncing letters and words correctly, but using the right intonation. So, when practising words and sentences, mimic the rising and falling intonation of native speakers.

The conversations in this book include questions to help guide you in your understanding. But you can go further by following some of these tips.

▶ Imagine the situation. When listening to or reading the conversations, try to imagine where the scene is taking place and who the main characters are. Let your experience of the world help you guess the meaning of the conversation, e.g. if a conversation takes place in a snack bar you can predict the kind of vocabulary that is being used.

▶ Concentrate on the main part. When watching a foreign film you usually get the meaning of the whole story from a few individual shots. Understanding a foreign conversation is similar. Concentrate on the main parts to get the message and don't worry about individual words.

▶ Guess the key words; if you cannot, ask or look them up.

▶ When there are key words you don't understand, try to guess what they mean from the context. If you cannot get the gist of a whole passage because of one word or phrase, try to repeat that word with a questioning tone; the speaker will probably paraphrase it, giving you the chance to understand it. If for example you wanted to find out the meaning of the word **molho** (*sauce*), you would ask **Que quer dizer molho?** or **O que é molho?**

7 SPEAKING

Rehearse in the foreign language. As all language teachers will assure you, successful learners are those who overcome their inhibitions and get into situations where they must speak, write and listen to the foreign language. Here are some useful tips to help you practise speaking Portuguese:

▶ Hold a conversation with yourself, using the conversations of the units as models and the structures you have learnt previously.

▶ After you have conducted a transaction with a salesperson, clerk or waiter in your own language, pretend that you have to do it in Portuguese, e.g. buying groceries, ordering food, drinks and so on.

▶ Look at objects around you and try to name them in Portuguese.

▶ Look at people around you and try to describe them in detail.

▶ Try to answer all of the questions in the book out loud.

▶ Say the dialogues out loud then try to replace sentences with ones that are true for you.

▶ Try to role-play different situations in the book.

▷ Don't let errors interfere with getting your message across. Making errors is part of any normal learning process, but some people get so worried that they won't say anything unless they are sure it is correct. This leads to a vicious circle as the less they say, the less practice they get and the more mistakes they make.

▷ Note the seriousness of errors. Many errors are not serious as they do not affect the meaning; for example if you use the wrong article (**o** for **a**) or the wrong pronouns (**ela fala** for **ele fala**). So concentrate on getting your message across and learn from your mistakes.

9 LEARN TO COPE WITH UNCERTAINTY

▷ **Don't over-use your dictionary.** When reading a text in the foreign language, don't be tempted to look up every word you don't know. Underline the words you do not understand and read the passage several times, concentrating on trying to get the gist of the passage. If, after the third time, there are still words which prevent you from getting the general meaning of the passage, look them up in the dictionary.

▷ **Don't panic if you don't understand.** If at some point you feel you don't understand what you are told, don't panic or give up listening. Either try and guess what is being said and keep following the conversation or, if you cannot, isolate the expression or words you haven't understood and have them explained to you. The speaker might paraphrase them and the conversation will carry on.

▷ **Keep talking.** The best way to improve your fluency in the foreign language is to talk every time you have the opportunity to do so: keep the conversations flowing and don't worry about the mistakes. If you get stuck for a particular word, don't let the conversation stop; paraphrase or replace the unknown word with one you do know, even if you have to simplify what you want to say. As a last resort use the word from your own language and pronounce it in the foreign accent.

Pronunciation guide

00.01

Here is a simple guide to the letters of the alphabet, their Portuguese name [in brackets], and how to pronounce them:

A [á] ah	B [bê] bay	C [cê] say	D [dê] day	E [é] eh	F [éfe] eff
G [guê] gay	H [agá] ah-gah	I [i] ee	J [jota] zhoh-tah	K [capa] cah-pah	L [éle] el
M [éme] em	N [éne] en	O [ó] oh	P [pê] pay	Q [quê] kay	R [érre] air
S [ésse] ess	T [tê] tay	U [ú] oo	V [vê] vay	W [dáblio] OR [vê duplo] dabble-yoo OR vay doo-ploo	X [xis] shish
Y [ípsilon OR i grego] ip-see-lon OR ee- gray-goo	Z [zê] zay				

Although the letters K, W and Y do not appear in Portuguese words, the letters exist for use in foreign words and abbreviations, and under the new spelling agreement (see later) have been incorporated into the alphabet proper. Listen to the whole alphabet on the audio a few times, then try to join in.

Most Portuguese words are pronounced as they are written – there are far fewer 'hidden' sounds or awkward sounds than in some other languages, such as English or French.

Once you have decoded a few tricky sounds, you should be able to have a go at reading Portuguese aloud as you see it. The following are some basic guidelines for some of the less straightforward pronunciation:

Portuguese letters	Pronunciation
ch	*sh*
lh	like the *lli* in *million*
nh	like the *ni* in *onion*
g, followed by **e** or **i**	like the *s* in *pleasure*
j	as above
h	always silent
x	tricky – varies from hard
	ks sound to a *z*, or even *sh*

Nasal sounds pronounced at the back of the nose are indicated by a ~ over the vowel, and also include words ending in **-m** or **-n**. Try to imagine saying them with a bad cold, when your nose is slightly blocked!

ão	*ow*
ãos	*owsh*
õe	*oy*
ões	*oysh*
ã	*ah*
ãs	*ahsh*
ãe	*eye*
ães	*eyesh*

One thing to remember is that when spoken words run together, there is an effect on the ending and beginning of the words involved, which may alter the sound from when a word is spoken in isolation from others. Also, regional variations, although fewer in Portugal than in some countries, do also alter sounds. The Algarve, in particular, is an area where the language can be difficult to work out at times.

The Portuguese alphabet is the same as the Roman one used in English, and other Latin-based languages.

A quick note here about the consonants **c**, **g** and **q**, which change their pronunciation depending on which vowels follow them. This can be a stumbling block for the uninitiated, hence a basic rule here:

▸ **c** before **a** / **o** / **u** = hard sound like *cat*
▸ **ç** (**c** + **cedilla** – see section on accents) before **a** / **o** / **u** = soft sound, like *face*
▸ **c** before **e** / **i** = soft
▸ **g** before **e** / **i** = soft, like the *s* sound in *treasure*
▸ **g** before **a** / **o** / **u** = hard, like in *goal*
▸ **g** + **u** before **e** / **i** = 'silent' **u** , e.g. **guitarra** *ghee* NOT *gwee*
▸ There are some exceptions (there always are!), such as **linguiça** (*spicy sausage*) = *lingwiça*.
▸ **q** is always followed by **u**
▸ **qu** before **e** / **i** = 'silent' **u**, e.g. **máquina** (*machine*) [*máKeena*, NOT *máKWeena*]; again there are some exceptions
▸ **qu** before **o** / **a** = *kw* e.g. **quadro** (*picture*) [*Kwadro*]
▸ **ph** does not exist in Portuguese: those words similar to English have an **f** – the same sound, but be careful with the spelling: e.g. **filósofo** = *philosopher*

BRAZILIAN SPELLING

After many years of wrangling over spelling throughout the Portuguese-speaking world (and most particularly between Portugal and Brazil), up-to-date orthographic (spelling) agreements are now being implemented under the new **Acordo Ortográfico**. However, there are still some differences in spelling between the two main variants of the language, Brazilian and Luso-African, which includes those African countries with Portuguese as an official language.

Be careful when using dictionaries – many of the bilingual editions available from UK and US publishers take Brazilian Portuguese as the standard and default to that when listing vocabulary options.

They usually put BP or PT after the word, and some remind you of common spelling changes at the foot of each page. Nevertheless, you still need to be on the ball to remember to look out for the differences – many of my own students end up using Brazilian words when they may never set foot in South America! Whilst this usually does not make too much difference, there may be an occasional variation in meaning which can lead to misunderstandings. If you can, eventually aim to work with a monolingual dictionary from either Portugal or Brazil, alongside your usual one. This will also help you improve your range of vocabulary.

ACCENTS

You will find the following written accents in Portuguese

´	Acute accent	Acento agudo	Opens vowel sound and indicates stress*	Gramática
^	Circumflex	Circunflexo	Closes vowel sound and indicates stress	português
~	Tilde	Til	Nasalizes vowel and usually indicates stress	amanhã
`	Grave accent	Acento grave	Opens vowel, non-stressing, indicates a contraction of two words	àquele = a + aquele

* Stress is the part of the word where you emphasize it when you say it.

There are also: **ç c cedilha** (*cedilla*), which makes the **c** soft, and the 'dieresis' **ü**, to denote words of foreign origin in their original forms (e.g. **Müller**).

Portuguese words are classified into three groups in terms of where the stress (emphasis) falls:

1 last syllable

2 penultimate (next to last)

3 antepenultimate (second to last)

The majority belong to Group 2 and do not usually require a written accent. The written accent occurs to enable words to be correctly stressed when they have deviated from the usual stress pattern. Whenever you see a written accent, that is where you should emphasize the word when you say it. Words also carry a written stress mark to distinguish them from a word with the same spelling but a different meaning, e.g. **por** (*by*) and **pôr** (*to put*). These are relatively rare.

A FEW TIPS TO HELP YOU ACQUIRE AN AUTHENTIC ACCENT

It is not absolutely vital to acquire a perfect accent. The aim is to be understood; here are a number of techniques for working on your pronunciation:

1 Listen carefully to the audio or native speaker or teacher. Whenever possible repeat out loud imagining you are a native speaker of Portuguese.

2 Record yourself and compare your pronunciation with that of a native speaker.

3 Ask native speakers to listen to your pronunciation and tell you how to improve it.

4 Ask native speakers how a specific sound is formed. Watch them and practise at home in front of a mirror.

5 Make a list of words that give you pronunciation trouble and practise them.

Now practise your pronunciation by repeating these place names, and look them up on the map of Portugal to see where they are.

First of all, the regions of Portugal:

1 Minho
2 Douro
3 Trás-os-Montes
4 Beira Alta
5 Beira Litoral
6 Beira Baixa
7 Estremadura
8 Ribatejo
9 Alentejo
10 Algarve

And some main cities:

1 Lisboa
2 Faro
3 Guarda
4 Setúbal
5 Coimbra
6 Porto
7 Braga
8 Évora
9 Portalegre
10 Vila Real

Useful expressions

hello	**olá** (casual)
good morning	**bom dia**
good afternoon	**boa tarde**
good evening	**boa tarde**
(after dark)	**boa noite**
good night	**boa noite**
goodbye	**adeus, tchau** (informal)
see you later	**até logo**
until tomorrow	**até amanhã**

COURTESIES

yes	**sim**
no	**não**
please	**se faz favor, faz favor, por favor**
thank you	**obrigado** (m) / **obrigada** (f)
you're welcome	**de nada / não tem de quê**
I'm sorry	**lamento, sinto muito** (to express regret) / **desculpe** (to apologize, to interrupt)
How are you?	**Como está?**
I'm fine	**estou bem**
And you?	**E o senhor / a senhora?** (formal to man / woman)
Are you OK?	**Tudo bem?** (informal)
excuse me	**com licença** (to get past)
that's fine / OK	**está bem**
sorry to bother you	**desculpe incomodar**
don't worry / it's not a problem	**não se preocupe**

Can you repeat, please?	**Pode repetir por favor?**
Could you speak more slowly?	**Podia falar mais devagar?**
Could you write it down?	**Podia escrevê-lo?**
Pardon / what did you say?	**Como?**
I'm sorry, I don't understand.	**Desculpe, não compreendo.**
I don't speak Portuguese very well.	**Não falo português muito bem.**
Do you speak English?	**Fala inglês?**
What does this mean?	**Que quer dizer isto?**
How do you say ... in English / Portuguese?	**Como se diz ... em inglês / português?**
Could you help me please?	**Podia ajudar-me por favor?**
Could you show me / give me ...?	**Podia mostrar-me / dar-me ...?**
May I / Can I ...?	**Posso ...?**

INTRODUCTIONS

My name is ...	**Chamo-me ...**
What is your name?	**Como se chama?**
I am English / American.	**Sou inglês (inglesa) / americano (americana).**
I'm thirty-five (years old).	**Tenho trinta e cinco anos.**
I am a (doctor).	**Sou médico (m) / médica (f).**
I am from (Oxford).	**Sou de Oxford.**
Pleased to meet you.	**Muito prazer.**
Likewise.	**Igualmente.**

EXPRESSING TASTE AND OPINION

I like ...	**Gosto de ...**
a little	**um pouco**
a lot	**muito**
immensely	**imenso**
not too much	**não muito**
I don't like ...	**Não gosto de ...**
I love ...	**Adoro ...**
I hate ...	**Detesto ...**
I think that ...	**Penso / Acho que ...**
I prefer ...	**Prefiro ...**

QUESTIONS

Who?	**Quem?**
What?	**(O) que?**
Which?	**Qual / Quais?**
When?	**Quando?**
How?	**Como?**
Why?	**Porquê?**
How much?	**Quanto?**
How many?	**Quantos / Quantas?**
Where?	**Onde?**

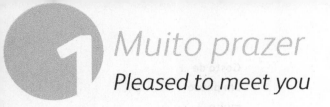

Muito prazer
Pleased to meet you

In this unit you will learn how to:
▶ *use basic greetings.*
▶ *ask and say how people are.*
▶ *ask and give names.*
▶ *use common courtesies.*

CEFR: (A2) *Can establish basic social contact by using the simplest everyday polite forms of: greetings and farewells; introductions; saying please, thank you and sorry.*

Greetings *Saudações*

Portuguese greetings are less fixed to the time of day than the corresponding English phrases. When saying hello to people during the day, **bom dia** (*good morning*) is used up until around 1.00 p.m., when many businesses close for lunch. **Boa tarde** (*good afternoon*) is used during the afternoon and into the early evening, at which point **boa noite** (*good evening*) takes over. A casual alternative is **olá** (*hi, hiya*). You will soon get an idea of when to use each greeting by listening to Portuguese people during their day-to-day routines. The words used to say hello are also used for taking leave and are often accompanied by **adeus** (*goodbye*), as in **adeus, boa noite**, and so on. **Tchau** came in on the crest of a wave from the popular Brazilian **telenovelas** (*soap operas*) and is also very casual.

 Can you work out the missing words in the list?

bom dia	*good _____, hello*
boa tarde	*good afternoon / evening, hello*
boa noite	*good _____, hello*
olá	*hi (hello)*
até logo	*see you later*
até já	*see you soon*
até amanhã	*see you tomorrow*

até à próxima	*see you next time*
tchau	_____
adeus	_____

01.01 **Now listen to these same words and expressions, then try to imitate the speaker's pronunciation.**

Diálogo 1

Paula meets a neighbour and briefly greets him.

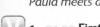

1 01.02 **First of all, listen to the key expressions:**

senhor Mendes	*Mr Mendes*
como está?	*how are you?*
estou bem	*I'm well*
obrigado	*thank you* (said by men)
obrigada	*thank you* (said by women)
e a senhora?	*and you madam?*

2 01.03 **Now listen to the conversation. What time of day is it?**

Paula	Bom dia, senhor Mendes. Como está?
Sr Mendes	Estou bem, obrigado, e a senhora?
Paula	Bem, obrigada.

Paula sees an acquaintance, Ana, approaching.

3 01.04 **Listen to the key expressions and try to repeat each one:**

está boa?	*are you well?* lit. *are you good?* (to a woman)
e	*and*
também	*also*
então	*well then / right then*

4 01.05 **Now listen to the conversation. What expressions does Paula use to say *goodbye*?**

Paula	Olá, Ana, está boa?
Ana	Estou, e a Paula?
Paula	Também estou, obrigada.
Ana	Então, até já.
Paula	Adeus, até logo.

Language discovery

1 THANK YOU

In this first dialogue you met **obrigado** and **obrigada**, both meaning *thank you*. **Obrigado** is used by men and **obrigada** by women: these are the masculine and feminine forms of the same word.

In Portuguese, the ending of words shows whether that word is masculine (usually an **-o** ending), or feminine (usually **-a**). You will learn more about this as you go along.

2 YOU

 What do you think was the difference between Mr Mendes calling Paula **'a senhora'**, and Ana using **'a Paula'**?

The Portuguese use a different word for *you* depending on how well you know the person, whether the person is in a higher social position, has senior work status, if they are older, and so on. In the dialogue you met two of the more formal words meaning *you*.

o senhor (man)	*you, lit. the gentleman / sir*
a senhora (woman)	*you, lit. the lady / madam*

You also heard a more informal way of saying *you*: **o** or **a** + the name of the person:

o Miguel	*you (to Miguel, masculine)*
a Paula	*you (to Paula, feminine)*

This is often used between colleagues or by older people to younger people.

You will learn more of these varied forms as you go along.

3 I AM, YOU ARE: TO BE

In the dialogue, people were asking and saying how they are, using:

estou	*I am*
está	*you are*

In English, *to be* is known as the infinitive of the verb. In Portuguese the equivalent infinitive is **estar**, *to be*. (This is the form of the verb you will find in a dictionary.)

The verb **estar** is used when talking about temporary feelings, states, characteristics and places.

4 QUESTIONS

In Portuguese, you can ask a simple question by raising your voice at the end of a sentence. There is usually no change in word order, as is often the case in English questions.

Está boa.   *You are well (to a woman).*

Está boa?   *Are you well? (lit. you are good?)*

Como está?   *How are you? (lit. how you are?)*

Practice 1

1 Can you figure out the missing words in this dialogue?

Ana	Boa noite, senhor Silva. Como _____?
Sr Silva	_____ bem, obrigado. E a senhora?
Ana	Estou _____, _____
Sr Silva	Então, boa _____ e _____ amanhã.
Ana	_____ noite.

2 What would you say to these people in the following situations?
   a meeting your friend Ana Paula mid-morning.
   b bumping into a business colleague at lunch time.
   c leaving a group of friends mid-afternoon – and you'll be seeing them again tomorrow.
   d popping into town to go shopping – you'll see your family later.
   e meeting your teacher in the evening.

3 Língua viva – At what part of the day is this new soap opera broadcast?

TV advert
Nova telenovela da TVI

Olá e Adeus!

Todas as manhãs

 Diálogo 2

Nuno asks Paula to a party, where she meets some people of her own age.

 1 01.06 **First listen to the new key expressions:**

estás bom?	*are you well? (to a man)*
e tu?	*and you?*
estou ótimo	*I'm fine (said by a man)*
desculpa	*excuse me*
como te chamas?	*what are you called?*
chamo-me	*I am called*
muito prazer	*pleased to meet you*
igualmente	*likewise*

2 01.07 **Now listen to the conversation and answer the questions.**
a What is Nuno's friend called?

Nuno	Boa noite, Miguel, estás bom?
Miguel	Estou, e tu?
Nuno	Estou ótimo, obrigado.
Miguel	*(turning to Paula)* Desculpa, como te chamas?
Paula	Chamo-me Paula, e tu?
Miguel	Miguel.
Paula	Muito prazer.
Miguel	Igualmente.

b Nuno asked Miguel '**estás bom?**'; what would he have said to Paula?

3 **Listen to the recording again and repeat the lines after the speakers.**

Language discovery

1 INFORMAL *YOU*

In Dialogue 2, the friends addressed each other by **tu**, which is the informal form of *you* – for friends, family and young people. The verb form also changed from **está** to **estás**.

está	*you are (formal)*
estás	*you are (informal)*

2 CHAMO-ME ... MY NAME IS ...

You will have noticed that when Paula was asked **Como te chamas?**, she responded with **chamo-me**. Don't worry at this stage about the varied position of the words **te** and **me**. Note that when asking the name of someone older, or whom you do not know very well, you use **como se chama?**, which is more formal.

3 DESCULPA EXCUSE ME

The word **desculpa** (or **desculpe** when used with strangers) can be used to mean *I'm sorry* in situations such as in Nuno's dialogue, as well as when interrupting a conversation, on approaching someone in the street to ask a question, or for apologizing if you have bumped into someone. You will also hear:

perdão	*sorry / I beg your pardon*
com licença	*excuse me (if you want to pass by)*

Possible responses include:

não faz mal	*don't worry*
com certeza	*of course*
faça / faz favor	*go ahead*

Practice 2

1 **You have just met Nuno in the street. Complete your conversation in Portuguese following the English prompts.**

Nuno	Boa tarde, como está?
You	**(a)** *Say hello. Tell him you're fine, thanks. Ask him how he is.*
Nuno	Estou bem, obrigado.
You	**(b)** *Say goodbye. Tell him you'll see him tomorrow.*
Nuno	Então, até à próxima.

2 01.08 **Now practise your part and listen to confirm your answers.**

3 What would you say to these people to find out their names?

a Ana Maria   **b** José   **c** Senhor Mendes

4 The following dialogue has become mixed up. Can you unscramble it? To help you get started the first line is **Bom dia, como está?**

Lúcia	Bem, obrigada.	____
Sr Silva	Eduardo.	____
Lúcia	Bom dia, como está?	_1_
Lúcia	Chamo-me Lúcia, e o senhor?	____
Sr Silva	Estou bem, obrigado, e a senhora?	____
Sr Silva	Igualmente.	____
Lúcia	Muito prazer.	____
Sr Silva	Desculpe, como se chama?	____

 Test yourself

1 Match the expressions with their meaning:

a	boa tarde	1	likewise
b	até à próxima	2	pleased to meet you
c	igualmente	3	good afternoon
d	bom dia	4	I'm sorry!
e	desculpe!	5	see you next time
f	muito prazer	6	good morning

2 Complete the sentences with the words from the box:

Como   próxima   e   muito   faz   me   chama   bem

- **a** até à _____
- **b** estou _____, obrigado
- **c** _____ está?
- **d** e _____ senhor?
- **e** Como se _____?
- **f** Chamo-_____ Maria.
- **g** _____ prazer
- **h** não _____ mal

SELF CHECK

I CAN...
... use basic greetings
... ask and say how people are
... ask and give names
... use common courtesies

1 Muito prazer *Pleased to meet you*   9

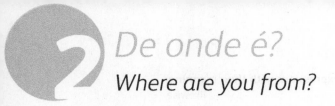

De onde é?

Where are you from?

In this unit you will learn how to:

▶ *ask where people are from.*
▶ *say where you are from.*
▶ *talk about nationalities.*

CEFR: (A2) *Can ask for and provide personal information;* **(A2)** *can answer simple questions and respond to simple statements in an interview.*

 Portuguese across the world

Portuguese is a language spoken in many continents, from **América do Sul** (*South America*), across **África** (*Africa*), and into **Ásia** (*Asia*), as well as in **Portugal continental** (*mainland Portugal*), which includes **a ilha da Madeira** (*the island of Madeira*) and **os Açores** (*the Azores*). **O Brasil** (*Brazil*), of course, has an enormous number of Portuguese speakers, and Brazilian soap operas are extremely popular in Portugal. The differences between Brazilian and European Portuguese are roughly akin to those between American and British English on pronunciation, vocabulary, and some points of grammar. You will hear **um brasileiro** (*a Brazilian*) later in this unit – listen carefully to his distinctive **sotaque** (*accent*).

 If you catch **a comboio** in Portugal, but it's a **trem** in Brazil, what do you think it is?
What about a Portuguese **autocarro**, which is an **ônibus** in Brazil?
And can you work out what both Brazilian **esporte** and Portuguese **desporto** happen to be?

Diálogo 1

A group of people have just met at a party. They are finding out where each other comes from.

1 02.01 **Listen to the key expressions first and try to repeat them as you go along.**

de onde é?	*where are you from?*
sou	*I am*
inglesa	*English (woman)*
sou de Londres	*I am from London*
português	*Portuguese (man)*

2 02.02 **Now listen to the dialogue and answer the questions.**

   a Where is Mr Pereira from?

Sr Pereira	Boa noite. Chamo-me Rui Pereira. E como se chama a senhora?
Isabel	Isabel.
Sr Pereira	Muito prazer, Isabel. De onde é?
Isabel	Sou inglesa; sou de Londres. E o senhor, de onde é?
Sr Pereira	Sou português, sou de Lisboa.

   b What is the Portuguese word for *London?*

Language discovery

1 MORE ABOUT *TO BE*

In Unit 1, you learnt **está** *you are* and **estou** *I am*, to talk about how people are feeling, using the verb **estar** (*to be*). The dialogues in this unit introduce you to another Portuguese verb *to be*: **ser**.

Why do you think there are two verbs meaning *to be*? Can you spot a difference in how they are used?

Sou de Portugal.	*I am from Portugal.*
De onde *é*?	*Where are you from?*
Susana *é* de Madrid.	*Susan is from Madrid.*
Pois, *somos* da Espanha.	*Well, we are from Spain.*
De onde *são*?	*Where are you* (pl) *from?*

Ser is generally used to describe more permanent characteristics, such as your nationality and where you come from.

This set of words (personal pronouns) indicates who is in play at any time – who is the subject of the verb. But these words are rarely used in Portuguese, because the ending of the verb (the action word) also shows the person in question:

sou	*I am*
eu sou	*I am*

The personal pronoun is useful for giving emphasis, e.g. **Sou da Espanha** *I'm from Spain*, but: **Eu sou da Espanha** *(As for me) I'm from Spain*, or when a particular verb ending may indicate one of a choice of people (**é** = *you are, she / he / it is*). You will learn more about verbs later. The full set of personal pronouns is:

Singular		Plural	
eu	*I*	**nós**	*we*
tu	*you (familiar)*	**vós**	*you (outdated, rarely used)*
ele	*he / it*	**eles**	*they (m)*
ela	*she / it*	**elas**	*they (f)*
o senhor (m) / a senhora (f)	*you (polite, formal)*	**os senhores (m) / as senhoras (f)**	*you (polite, formal)*
você	*you (semi-formal)*	**vocês**	*you*

3 NATIONALITY

In Unit 1 you learnt that certain words in Portuguese have either a masculine or feminine ending, depending on whom (or what) that word is referring to. The same is true of words describing people's nationality. Also, if you are talking about more than one person, you must remember to change the word into a plural one. This sounds rather complex, but in fact, once you have got used to the idea, it is very logical, and with practice it becomes second nature.

Look at the table and compare the singular and plural forms of the nationalities:

Listen now to some of the words for nationality, and repeat each one as you hear them.

Name of country	Masculine singular	Masculine plural	Feminine singular	Feminine plural
Os Estados Unidos *USA*	americano	americanos	americana	americanas
O Brasil *Brazil*	brasileiro	brasileiros	brasileira	brasileiras
A Inglaterra *England*	inglês	ingleses	inglesa	inglesas
Portugal	português	portugueses	portuguesa	portuguesas
A Alemanha *Germany*	alemão	alemães	alemã	alemãs
A Espanha *Spain*	espanhol	espanhóis	espanhola	espanholas

Like **americano** are: **italiano** (*Italian*), **grego** (*Greek*), **australiano** (*Australian*).

Like **inglês** are: **irlandês** (*Irish*), **francês** (*French*), **chinês** (*Chinese*), **escocês** (*Scottish*).

If you have two or more males, you will use the masculine plural, similarly, a group of women will need the feminine plural. However, should you have a mixed group, the masculine plural is applied.

Notice that the names of countries can be masculine (**o**) or feminine (**a**). Some countries, such as Portugal itself, are neither. This is just an anomaly in the language – you have to get used to them! The USA is plural (**os**), as it refers to the group of states.

o Brasil	*Brazil*
a Itália	*Italy*
os Estados Unidos	*the United States*
Sou alemã.	*I am German. (f.)*
É inglês?	*Are you English?*
Tom é escocês.	*Tom is Scottish.*

1   **Match the correct form of nationality to the description of the people:**

   a Mary and John are English.   1 americano
   b Sofia is Italian.   2 portugueses
   c Bill is an American.   3 italiana
   d Connie and Theresa are from Ireland.   4 irlandesas
   e Carmen is a Spanish lady.   5 escocês
   f The people who live in Portugal.   6 ingleses
   g Jock comes from Scotland.   7 espanhola

2   **Complete what the following people are saying about their nationalities and where they are from.**

a

Maria

b

O sr / a sra Schmidt

c

Ellen / Mary

d

Sandra, John, Brenda

Marco Giovanni

Mac

3 Now write sentences about the same people (a–f), using the correct part of **ser** (*to be*). It is common practice in Portugal to use **o** (masculine) / **a** (feminine) before people's names, hence the first example would read:

A Maria é de Portugal.   *Maria is from Portugal.*

É portuguesa.   *She is Portuguese.*

You could use the word for **ela** (*she*) here, for emphasis.

Ela é portuguesa.

Now try the rest. You could use **ele** (*he*) or **eles / elas** (*they*).

 Diálogo 2

David has just met someone and he is trying to start a conversation.

 1 02.04 **Listen to the key expressions first:**

mas	*but*
fala ...?	*do you speak ...?*
falo ...	*I speak ...*
sim	*yes*
um pouco de	*a bit of*
não	*no / not*
fala bem	*you speak well*
bem	*well*

2 02.05 **Now listen to the conversation. What nationality is the man?**

David	Bom dia. Desculpe, mas fala inglês?
João	Não, não falo. O senhor é inglês?
David	Sim, sou. Falo um pouco de português. Mas, o senhor é português?
João	Não, não sou.
David	Mas fala bem português.
João	Sou brasileiro!

3 **Replay the dialogue, pausing to repeat after each line.**

Language discovery

1 SAYING YES AND NO

To say something negative, you place the word **não** before the verb:

Não sou italiana. *I am not Italian.*

Não falo chinês. *I do not speak Chinese.*

Note there is no Portuguese equivalent of the word *do* in this second sentence. On answering a question, you may hear the double negative, as in the dialogue:

não, não falo *no, I do not speak*

The word for *yes* is **sim**:

Sim, falo OR **Falo, sim** *Yes, I (do) speak …*

Both **não** and **sim** are nasalized – i.e. they should be pronounced at the back of the nose. This takes some practice for English speakers, so keep trying! See the Pronunciation guide for more on this, and try to imitate the sounds you hear on the audio.

2 LANGUAGES

The name of a language is the same as the masculine word of nationality, hence **italiano** can mean *the Italian language*, *an Italian man*, or simply *Italian*, eg. **vinho italiano** (*Italian wine*). A German woman could say:

Sou alemã, falo alemão. *I'm German (a German woman), I speak German.*

Practice 2

1 How would you do the following?

a Ask someone if they speak Italian.
b Say you are not American.
c Say you speak Portuguese and English.
d Ask someone if they speak Portuguese.
e Say you are not German, but you speak German.

2 Decide whether these statements about which languages people speak are true (V = verdadeiro) or false (F = falso). Assume each person only speaks one of the native languages of their home country!

a A Sara é dos Estados Unidos. Fala alemão.
b O Marco fala italiano; é da Itália.
c Eu sou do Brasil, falo português.
d A senhora Brown é da Inglaterra. Fala inglês.
e O senhor Schmidt fala alemão. É português.

3 Língua viva – Study the graph and answer the questions:

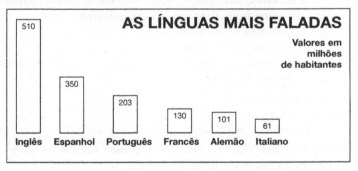

AS LÍNGUAS MAIS FALADAS

Valores em milhões de habitantes

| Inglês | Espanhol | Português | Francês | Alemão | Italiano |
| 510 | 350 | 203 | 130 | 101 | 61 |

a Which language is most widely spoken?
b Which two languages are the least spoken?

3 02.06 **An entrevistador (*interviewer*) is conducting a survey about languages and nationalities. You decide to participate. Follow the prompts to complete the dialogue.**

Entrevistador	Boa tarde. Desculpe, mas fala português?
You	**(a)** *Say yes, you speak a little bit.*
Entrevistador	É da Alemanha?
You	**(b)** *Say no, you're not German, and give your nationality.*
Entrevistador	Então (*well then*), fala inglês?
You	**(c)** *Say yes, you speak English, and also Italian.*
Entrevistador	Fala bem português.
You	**(d)** *Say thank you, and goodbye.*

4 Which languages are spoken at this shop?

> AQUI FALA-SE
> INGLÊS,
> PORTUGUÊS,
> ALEMÃO

5 Read the following dialogue, in which Mr Pereira asks a couple where they come from, then answer the questions:

Sr Pereira	Boa noite. De onde são os senhores?
Susana	Somos da Espanha. Somos espanhóis.
Mário	A Susana é de Madrid, e eu sou de Barcelona. E o senhor, de onde é?
Sr Pereira	Pois, sou de Portugal!

  a What time of day is it?
  b Where is the man from?
  c What are the verbs for: *I am, you* (plural) *are, we are?*

6 Now look at the following dialogue and work out the missing words, according to the English prompts:

Sra Fernandes	**(a)** _____ (*good morning*). De onde **(b)** _____ (*are you*) a senhora?
Angelika	**(c)** _____ (*I am*) da Grécia; sou **(d)** _____ (*Greek*). E a senhora, **(e)** _____ (*where are you from*)?
Sra Fernandes	Pois, sou **(f)** _____ (*Portuguese*), sou **(g)** _____ (*from*) Tavira.

1 Can you remember how to do these things in Portuguese?

  a Ask Paulo where he's from.
  b Say which country you are from.
  c Ask Senhor Mendes if he is Brazilian.
  d Ask where Mr and Mrs Oliveira come from.
  e Speak on behalf of yourself and a friend, giving your nationality.
  f Say that Júlia is Portuguese.
  g Ask if João is from the USA.
  h Ask someone if they speak English.
  i Say no, you don't speak German.
  j Say yes, you are English.

2 What comes before the following words: o, os, a, as or X (nothing)?

  a _____ Espanha
  b _____ Cristina
  c _____ Brasil
  d _____ Miguel
  e _____ Estados Unidos
  f _____ senhoras
  g _____ Portugal
  h _____ senhor

3 02.07 **Listen to some words of nationalities and select what you hear.**

a	brasileiro	brasileira	brasileiros
b	espanhol	espanhóis	espanholas
c	alemão	alemães	alemã
d	grega	gregos	grego
e	chinesa	chinesas	chineses
f	francesas	francês	franceses

SELF CHECK

	I CAN...
○	. . . ask where people are from
○	. . . say where I am from
○	. . . talk about nationalities

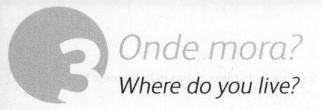

3 Onde mora?

Where do you live?

In this unit you will learn how to:
▶ talk about where you live.
▶ recognize addresses.
▶ talk about where you work.
▶ ask other people about where they live and work.
▶ use numbers 0–20.

CEFR: (A1) *Can describe him / herself, what he / she does and where he / she lives;* **(A1)** *can handle numbers.*

 Addresses

You may have noticed abbreviations on address plates in Portugal, for example the number of the floor in apartment blocks – **3°**, **2°** and so on, meaning *third, second*, etc. Other common abbreviations to look out for are **R. (rua** = *road / street*), **r/c (rés-do-chão** = *ground floor*), **Av. (avenida** = *avenue*), **Pr. (praça** = *square*), **esq. (esquerda** = *left*), **dir. (direita** = *right*). Many streets are named after famous historical or military heroes, or dates of historical events, such as **Praça de Camões** (named after Portugal's national poet) or **25 de Abril** (*25 April* – when the 1974 revolution took place).

There is a variety of situations in which you may have to talk about where people live; it could be an informal conversation, you may be filling in forms, or you may need someone's address in order to pay them a visit. There are two verbs in Portuguese which mean to live: **morar** has close associations with **morada**, meaning *address* and the notion of residence; you will also come across the verb **viver**, used in a more general sense of living, such as in a region or country.

a Can you figure out this address:
   Avenida 5 de Outubro, 25, 3° dir., Lisboa.
b In what order do the details of the address appear?

Diálogo 1

Ana is finding out where different people live.

1 03.01 **Listen to and repeat the new expressions:**

mora	*you live, he, she lives*
moro	*I live*
em	*in*
na	*on / in (the)*
a avenida	*(the) avenue*
na Avenida da República	*on Republic Avenue*
aqui	*here*
moram	*they / you (pl) live*
a praça	*(the) square*
agora	*now*
vive	*he / she lives, you live*

2 03.02 **Now read and listen to the dialogue. Can you work out where José lives now?**

Ana	Boa noite, senhor Mendes. Onde mora?
Sr Mendes	Moro em Lisboa, na Avenida da República. E a Ana, mora em Lisboa?
Ana	Não, moro aqui em Albufeira. Onde moram o senhor e a senhora Silva?
Sr Mendes	Moram no Porto, na Praça São Vicente. Onde mora o José?
Ana	O José? Pois, agora vive no Brasil.

Language discovery

1 HOW TO SAY *THE*

You have already learnt about the idea of masculine and feminine words, and you have seen the words **o** and **a** used with certain countries, and with people's names. In the dialogue, these words are used to describe where people live:

a avenida	*the avenue*
a praça	*the square*

Everything – that is all objects, people, animals, concepts – in the Portuguese language is either masculine or feminine. Most masculine words end in **-o**, and most feminine ones, like the examples above, end in **-a**.

Likewise the words for *the* are **o** for masculine words, and **a** for feminine words. As you progress you will find many words do not fit the **-o / -a** ending structure, so you will have to learn from the vocabulary lists or glossary which group they belong to.

To form the plural *the*, (i.e. when talking about more than one object) just add an **-s** to both the word for *the* and the noun (the object itself); there are some irregular plural nouns for which you'll learn the rules as you progress.

as avenidas *the avenues*

Wherever helpful, words will be presented with the **o** or **a**, or (m) or (f) in the rest of this course.

 How would you form the plural of these words: **a rua, o dia, a senhora?**

2 HOW TO SAY *IN* AND *ON*

The word for describing *in* or *on*, is **em**, as seen in **moro *em* Lisboa**. However, when you follow this word by any of the words for *the*, the words join together to form a contraction.

 Do you think **na praça** (*in the square*) is masculine or feminine? And what do you think **nos** is, masculine or feminine, singular or plural?

So, the contractions are as follows:

em + o / a	= **no / na**
in + the (masculine / feminine)	= *in / on the*
em + a praça	= *in + the square*
na praça	= *in the square*

and in the plural,

em + os / as	**= nos / nas**
in + the (m / f plural)	*= in / on the (plural)*
em + as avenidas	*= in + the avenues*
nas avenidas	*= in the avenues*

Up to now, you have been using parts of the two verbs **ser / estar** (*to be*) to talk about different aspects of people. You learnt in Unit 2 how to use parts of the verb **falar** (*to speak*) and now you have been introduced to the verbs **morar / viver** (*to live*). Many verbs follow the same pattern of endings as **falar**, as the **-ar** ending is the most common in Portuguese.

Compare **falar**, **morar** and **trabalhar** (*to work*) which you will use later in this chapter:

	falar *to speak*	morar *to live*	trabalhar *to work*
I	fal**o**	mor**o**	trabalh**o**
you (informal/ familiar)	fal**as**	mor**as**	trabalh**as**
he, she, it you (formal)	fal**a**	mor**a**	trabalh**a**
we	fal**amos**	mor**amos**	trabalh**amos**
they you (plural)	fal**am**	mor**am**	trabalh**am**

It takes the same verb form as *he / she*.

Unless you are speaking to family, close friends, or children, use the *you* verb forms with the **-a** ending when talking to just one person.

Can you spot the similar patterns? It is the continued presence of the letter **a**, brought down from the initial **-ar** ending.

Practice 1

1 **Complete the sentences with the correct part of the verb morar, and the correct form of em / no / na (*in / on the*) to match the places mentioned.**

   a Lúcia (*she*) _____ _____ Avenida 25 de Abril.
   b Nós (*we*) _____ _____ Rua Silvestre.
   c Eu (*I*) _____ _____ Lisboa.
   d Eles (*they*) _____ _____ Praça de Camões
   e Tu (*you*) _____ _____ Braga.

2 **So, now have a go. How do you do the following?**

   a Ask Senhora Gomes where she lives.
   b Say that you live in England.
   c Say that Maria lives in the square.
   d Ask where Senhor and Senhora Neto live.
   e Ask Renato if he lives in Germany.

Listening and reading

João is giving his address in an email, describing exactly where he lives.

1   03.03 **Listen to the new words first:**

o número	*number*
o apartamento	*the apartment, flat*
fica	*is situated*
o terceiro	*third*
o andar	*floor*
à esquerda	*on the left*

2 Now listen to João, then answer the questions:

  a In which city and region of Portugal does João live?

  b What is the name of the street where he lives?

  c Which floor and which side is his apartment?

Moro em Silves no Algarve, na Rua Samora Barros, número seis, e o apartamento fica no terceiro andar, à esquerda.

3 Now listen to and read Marília's email reply. You will hear the new words first.

numa casa antiga	*in an old house*
o segundo	*second*
à direita	*on the right*
número quinze	*number fifteen*

4 When you have read and heard the passage, answer the questions:

  a In which city does Marília live?

  b Does she live on an avenue or on a square?

Eu vivo em Portugal, em Lisboa. Vivo numa casa antiga na Praça de Camões, número quinze, segundo andar, à direita.

Language discovery

1 OS NÚMEROS *NUMBERS*

You cannot get very far without numbers, in any language, as they
creep into so many daily transactions – addresses, time, money,
quantities – so you must start now to build up a good grasp of them.
Let's start with 0–20.

 03.07 **Listen to the numbers and repeat them out loud before you
look at them.**

0	**zero**	7	**sete**	14	**catorze**
1	**um, uma**	8	**oito**	15	**quinze**
2	**dois, duas**	9	**nove**	16	**dezasseis**
3	**três**	10	**dez**	17	**dezassete**
4	**quatro**	11	**onze**	18	**dezoito**
5	**cinco**	12	**doze**	19	**dezanove**
6	**seis**	13	**treze**	20	**vinte**

Numbers one and two have both a masculine and a feminine form – so if
you are talking about *two houses*, it's **duas casas**.

Practise your numbers every day for at least a week, and test yourself by
counting backwards, or asking someone to test you out loud.

2 1ST, 2ND, 3RD ...

 03.08 **Listen carefully to the following numbers on the audio and
repeat each one, imitating the pronunciation of the presenter.**

1st	**primeiro**	4th	**quarto**
2nd	**segundo**	5th	**quinto**
3rd	**terceiro**		

You will learn further ones as you go along.

 Look at the expression **a terceira casa** *the third house*. Why do you think
terceira has an **-a** ending? How would you say *the first square*?

These words are not only used for talking about floors in a building, you
will also find them in Unit 7 on days of the week, and Unit 11 on directions.

3 HOW TO SAY A OR AN

The words for number *one* (**um**, **uma**) are also the masculine and feminine forms of the words for *a* / *an*. Therefore, you can talk in terms of **uma casa** (*a house*) or **um apartamento** (*an apartment*). Remember always to check in the Portuguese–English vocabulary to see whether the word is masculine or feminine. This is referred to as the word's gender. If you are using a dictionary, then the word will usually be followed by (m) or (f). If there is no indication of gender, it is because the word follows the standard pattern: **-o** / **-a** ending.

4 HOW TO SAY IN A OR ON A

In Marília's email, you came across the expression **vivo numa casa antiga** (*I live in an old house*). This is another example of a contracted structure, just like the **no** / **na** you learnt in Unit 2. Here you have: **em + um** / **uma**, becoming **num** and **numa**.

5 WORDS FOR DESCRIBING

Words that describe things (adjectives), such as **antigo** (*old*), are usually placed after the word they are describing. They also have to have the same appropriate masculine or feminine ending, and must be either singular or plural. This is called 'agreeing'. Therefore *a modern apartment* would be **um apartamento moderno**.

 Look at the expression **um edifício alto** (*a tall building*); is that masculine or feminine? If *an old house* is **uma casa antiga**, what would *two old houses be*?

 Practice 2

1 **Língua viva – Look at the two address cards. Which is Senhor Mendes's, whose establishment is on the ground floor, on a street?**

Pastelaria Snack Bar **ANTIQUA** Aberto das 7:30 às 21:30h. Encerra ao Sábado. **Rua Dr. Augusto E. Nunes, 40 r/c • Tel. 29698**	Café-Restaurante **O AVENIDA** • Cozinha Regional • Petiscos • Com nova sala de refeições Aberto das 7 às 23h. Encerra aos Domingos. Av. São Sebastião, 25 • Tel. 33872

2 **The following people have got lost. Look at the descriptions they give of where they live, and match them up with the address plates:**

a.

Praça de S.Jorge
Nº 6

1

Moro num apartamento moderno numa praça. Fica no terceiro andar, à direita.

b.

Rua do Ouro
Nº 11

2

Moro na Rua do Ouro, número dezasseis, segundo andar.

c.

PRAÇA
LISBOA 56
3 DIR

3

Moro na Praça de São Jorge numa casa moderna, número seis.

d.

Rua do Ouro
16 , 2º

4

Moro na Rua do Ouro, número onze; é uma casa antiga.

e.

Praça de S.
Jorge 13-5' Esq

5

Moro na Praça de São Jorge, número treze, quinto andar, à esquerda.

Diálogo 2

1 03.09 **Paulo and Maria are talking about where they work. Listen to the new expressions first:**

onde trabalha?	*where do you work?*
onde é que trabalha?	*where is it that you work?*
trabalho	*I work*
o que faz?	*what do you do?*

2 03.10 **Now listen to the dialogue and answer the questions.**

Paulo	Maria, onde é que trabalha?
Maria	Trabalho em Faro, no aeroporto.
Paulo	E o que faz?
Maria	Trabalho no check-in. E o Paulo, onde trabalha?
Paulo	Sou banqueiro; trabalho num banco em Tavira.

   a Where does Maria work?
   b What does Paulo do?

Language discovery

1 ONDE (É QUE ...)? *WHERE (IS IT THAT ...)?*

You will often hear Portuguese people inserting the expression **é que** into questions, usually to pad out or emphasize what they are saying. So you could say **onde é que mora?** (*where is it that you live?*) or **onde mora?**, as well as **onde é que trabalha?** (*where is it that you work?*) or **onde trabalha?**

2 PROFISSÕES *PROFESSIONS*

When someone asks you **onde trabalha?**, or **o que faz?**, there are two ways you could answer, as Maria and Paulo did in the dialogue. When you are describing your place of work, don't forget the contractions **num**, **numa**, **no** and **na**.

So, you could say:

	num banco		*in a bank*
	numa escola		*in a school*
Trabalho	**num escritório**	*I work*	*in an office*
	numa empresa		*in a business*
	na universidade		*in the university*
	no banco Espírito Santo		*in the Espírito Santo bank*

OR,

	professor / professora		teacher
	estudante (m / f)		student
Sou	escritor / escritora	I am a	writer
	médico / médica		doctor
	enfermeiro / enfermeira		nurse
	advogado / advogada		lawyer

So, *a male teacher* is **um professor**, *a female doctor* is **uma médica**, but *a student* can be either **um** or **uma estudante**.

You may be **uma dona de casa** (*a housewife*) or a **homem / mulher de negócios** (*businessman / woman*), or you may not work, **não trabalho** (*I do not work*), **estou reformado/a** (*I'm retired*), **estou desempregado/a** (*I'm unemployed*).

With names of professions, the Portuguese do not use the word *a*, they say literally *I am teacher*, etc.

 Practice 3

1 Work out how to do the following:
   a Ask senhor Gomes where he works.
   b Say that you are a student.
   c Ask José what he does for a living.
   d Say where you work.
   e Say that you do not work.

2 Complete the sums, choosing from the words in the box.

treze   dezanove   dezoito   cinco   dois   doze

   a dois + três   = _____
   b vinte – oito   = _____
   c dezassete – quatro   = _____
   d nove + nove   = _____
   e dez – oito   = _____
   f quinze + quatro   = _____

3 Match the people to where they work.

a	Sou estudante.	**1**	empresa
b	Sou banqueiro.	**2**	escritório
c	Sou mulher de negócios.	**3**	aeroporto
d	Trabalho no check-in.	**4**	universidade
e	Sou secretária.	**5**	escola
f	Sou professora.	**6**	banco

Test yourself

1 Work out how to say the following:
  a I work in a school.
  b Where do you live? (to Mr and Mrs Pereira)
  c I live in the square.
  d She is a teacher.
  e We live in a modern house.
  f Where do you work? (to one person, polite)
  g What do you do? (to one person, polite)

2 Complete the sentences with words from the box.

no numa no na num no

  a Trabalho _____ Banco Santander.
  b Tu trabalhas _____ universidade?
  c Mora _____ casa antiga.
  d Trabalham _____ hospital.
  e Moramos _____ Avenida Principal.
  f O José trabalha _____ aeroporto de Lisboa.

3 Use what you know to answer these questions about yourself.
You may need to check in a dictionary how to describe your job.
  a Como se chama?
  _____
  b Onde mora?
  _____
  c O que faz?
  _____
  d Onde trabalha?
  _____

SELF CHECK

I CAN...
. . . talk about where I live
. . . recognize addresses
. . . talk about where I work
. . . ask other people about where they live and work
. . . use numbers 0–20

A família
The family

In this unit you will learn how to:
▶ *point people out.*
▶ *describe your family.*
▶ *talk about age.*

CEFR: (A2) *Can establish social contact: introductions;* **(A2)** *can ask for and provide personal information.*

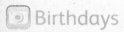

Birthdays

To say how old somebody is, the Portuguese say how many years someone has. **Tenho 23 anos** is how you say *I am 23 years old*. To ask someone how old they are, you say **Quantos anos tem?** Having a birthday, is known as **fazer anos** (lit. *to make years*). **Quando faz anos?** *When is your birthday?* (lit. *When do you make years?*). To talk about your birthday, you also refer to your **dia de anos** (*birthday*). If you want to congratulate someone on their birthday, say **Parabéns!** *Congratulations!*

If you are lucky enough to be invited to **uma festa de anos** (*a birthday party*) or other **celebração** (*celebration*), be prepared for a wonderful feast! It is typical for birthday meals to be held in restaurants, where the waiters will emerge carrying the **bolo** (*cake*), complete with its **velas** (*candles*), and everyone in the restaurant usually joins in a rousing chorus of **parabéns a você** (*happy birthday to you*).

Using the information above, how would you say *I am eighteen*?

Diálogo 1

Senhor Moura is pointing out his family to a friend while at a party.

1 04.01 **Listen to, and repeat the key expressions first.**

cá	*here*
sozinho	*alone*
com	*with*
a minha família	*my family*
este é o meu filho	*this is my son*
esta é a minha filha	*this is my daughter*
mais velha	*eldest (f)*
aquela (f)	*that*
ali	*there, over there*
quem?	*who?*
aquele (m)	*that*

2 04.02 **Now listen to the conversation; what Portuguese word is used for *wife*?**

Alexandra	Boa tarde, Senhor Moura. Está cá sozinho?
Sr Moura	Não, estou com a minha família. Este é o meu filho Roberto, e esta é a minha filha mais velha, Sónia.
Alexandra	Muito prazer. E a senhora Moura?
Sr Moura	Pois, a minha mulher é aquela senhora ali.
Alexandra	E quem é aquele senhor ali?
Sr Moura	É o nosso chefe!

Language discovery

1 ESTE / AQUELE *THIS / THAT*

You should have noticed the different words used in the dialogue for pointing out people. **Este** (m) / **esta** (f) is used for people, or things near to you, and **aquele** (m) / **aquela** (f) for those at a distance. To talk about more than one person or thing, just add an **-s**, to make the plurals *these* and *those*.

este	**esta**	**estes**	**estas**	*this / these*
aquele	**aquela**	**aqueles**	**aquelas**	*that / those*

aquelas senhoras	*those women*
estes senhores	*these men*

When talking about a possession (this includes family members) you must make sure that the word you use for *my*, *your* and so on agrees (matches) with the object in possession. If this does not seem logical at first, it may help you to remember that these words describe possession in some way, and that, as you have already learnt in Unit 2, descriptive words (adjectives) agree with the word they describe. Here are some of the possessive words you are going to need:

	masculine	feminine
my	o meu	a minha
your (singular, polite)	o seu	a sua
our	o nosso	a nossa

Even though you may be a man talking about your daughter, you would use the feminine word for *my*. Look at these examples:

o **meu** marido   a **minha** mulher

o **seu** bolo   a **sua** festa

o **nosso** filho   a **nossa** filha

To talk about more than one possessed object (i.e. in the plural), add an **-s** to the appropriate words.

os meus amigos   *my (male) friends*

as nossas filhas   *our daughters*

Did you notice in each case the word for *the* (**o**, **a**, **os**, **as**) is also included? So what you actually end up saying is *the, my*, and so on. This is just a quirk of the language. Don't worry. All languages are full of them!

3 MAIS OU MENOS *MORE OR LESS*

When describing someone who is older, younger, taller, smaller, etc., you need the words **mais** (*more*) and **menos** (*less*) used with the appropriate adjective. So you can have combinations such as:

mais velho	*older (more old)*	**o mais velho**	*the oldest*
mais novo	*younger (more young)*	**o mais novo**	*the youngest*
mais alto	*taller (more tall)*	**o mais alto**	*the tallest*
mais baixo	*shorter (more short)*	**o mais baixo**	*the shortest*

You can also use **menos velho** (*less old*), etc.

Don't forget to make the adjectives agree. A girl who is *younger* will be **mais nova**, and boys who are the *tallest* will be **os mais altos**. The words should appear after the person or thing they refer to:

o filho mais alto   *the tallest son*

as senhoras mais velhas   *the oldest ladies*

4 A FAMÍLIA *THE FAMILY*

 04.03 **Here are the words for basic family relationships. Listen and imitate the pronunciation of the speaker.**

o filho	*son*
o irmão	*brother*
a filha	*daughter*
a irmã	*sister*
o marido	*husband*
o pai	*father*
a mulher	*wife*
a mãe	*mother*

The plural of **filho** – **filhos** – can mean *sons* or *children*.

 ## Practice 1

 1   Make sentences about family relationships using the prompts in brackets.

   a Este é _____. (*my brother*)
   b Aquela é _____. (*our mother*)
   c Esta é _____. (*your daughter*)
   d Estes são _____. (*our sons*)
   e Aquele é _____. (*my father*)

2   How would you say the following?

   a Ana is the youngest daughter.
   b Miguel is our tallest brother.
   c They are my older sons.
   d António is shorter.
   e Maria and Paula are taller.

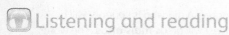

Listening and reading

1 04.04 **Listen to senhor Moura describing his family; you will hear the key expressions first.**

tenho	I have
bastante	quite
pequena (f)	small
(a) escola secundária	secondary / high school
muito	very
simpática (f)	nice
elegante	elegant
temos	we have
os outros	the other(s)
desportivo	sporty
calma (f)	calm, easygoing

2 04.05 **Now listen to and read the passage, then answer the question: How many children does Mr Moura have?**

Tenho uma família bastante pequena. A minha mulher chama-se Rosa e é professora. Trabalha numa escola secundária em Braga. Ela é muito simpática e elegante. Temos três filhos: a Sónia, que é a mais velha, e a Catarina, a irmã, e o Roberto, o filho mais novo. A Sónia trabalha num hospital, e os outros dois são estudantes. O Roberto é alto e desportivo, e a Catarina é muito calma.

3 Answer these questions in Portuguese about the família Moura.

a Como se chama a esposa do (*of*) senhor Moura?
b Onde é que ela trabalha?
c Quem é o filho mais novo?
d Como é a Catarina? (*What is Catarina like?*)
e O que faz a Sónia?
f O Roberto é baixo?

4 04.06 **Now listen to the audio and check your answers.**

Language discovery

This is an important verb for you to learn, as you will be using it in many situations. The main parts you need to know are:

ter	to have
tenho	*I have*
tens	*you have (informal)*
tem	*you (singular) have, he / she / it has*
temos	*we have*
têm	*you (pl) have, they have*

You learnt that **Quantos anos tem?** means *How old are you?* Which word in Portuguese actually means *do you have*? How would you ask *Do you have children?*

2 DESCRIBING PEOPLE

Senhor Moura described his family, using adjectives, to tell you about their characteristics. He used the words **simpático** (*nice*), **elegante** (*elegant*), **desportivo** (*sporty*), and **calmo** (*calm*). There are many words you can use to describe people. Remember to make them agree with the person you are describing, by changing the final **-o**, to **-a** (masc. → fem).

Words ending in **-e** are the same for both masculine and feminine.

Have a go at working out the missing meanings in this list.

arrogante	_____
tímido/a	_____
sério/a	_____
engraçado/a	*funny*
preguiçoso/a	*lazy*
barulhento/a	*noisy*
orgulhoso/a	*proud*
alegre	_____
artístico/a	_____
honesto/a	_____

In Units 1 and 2, you met two ways of expressing *I am*, etc. in Portuguese. One is using the verb **ser** (for more permanent characteristics) and the other with the verb **estar** (when situations are more temporary). In the Reading passage, Senhor Moura described the characteristics of his family members using **ser**, but if he had wanted to say how someone was at the moment, he would have used **estar**.

How would you say *He is fat* (**gordo**) – i.e. *he is a fat person* / *He is fat* (at the moment)?

It's important to think carefully before you use these verbs, but you'll get lots of practice as you progress through this course. Let's just check you know the parts of the two verbs:

ser	
sou	*I am*
és	*you are (informal)*
é	*you are, he / she / it is*
somos	*we are*
são	*you (pl) are, they are*

estar	
estou	*I am*
estás	*you are (informal)*
está	*you are, he / she / it is*
estamos	*we are*
estão	*you (pl) are, they are*

1 How would you say the following in Portuguese?

   a Do you (sing / formal) have a daughter?

   b We have two children.

   c Does she have a brother?

   d I have a sister.

   e Do you (pl) have children?

2 Complete the missing letters in these words for describing people. Give the masculine form for each.

   a pr__gu__ço__o

   b e__eg__nt__

   c d__sp__rt__vo

   d __ar__lh__nt__

   e s__ri__

   f c__lm__

   g n__rv__so

   h __on__st__

3 Língua viva – What type of person is this shop looking to employ?

ADMISSÃO
PARA FOTÓGRAFOS

Idade até 25 anos, não estudante, artístico, disponibilidade imediata

HOJE TELEF.: 813 91 74

 Diálogo 2

1 04.07 **Senhor Moura is being asked about the ages of his children. Listen to the key expressions first.**

quantos anos tem o seu filho?	*how old is your son?*
(os) anos	*years*
ora bem	*well now*

2 04.08 **Now listen to the conversation and answer the question: how old is Sónia?**

Tânia	Senhor Moura, quantos anos tem o seu filho mais novo?
Sr Moura	O mais novo, o Roberto, tem quinze anos.
Tânia	E as suas filhas?
Sr Moura	Pois, a Catarina tem dezassete anos e a Sónia vinte.
Tânia	E o senhor? Quantos anos tem?
Sr Moura	Eu? Ora bem, eu tenho ...!

Practice 3

1 **Provide the correct form of este (*this*) or aquele (*that*) for each sentence.**

a (*this*) _____ é o meu pai.

b (*that*) _____ é a minha mulher.

c (*these*) _____ são as nossas amigas.

d (*this*) _____ é a sua irmã?

e (*those*) _____ são os nossos filhos.

2 04.09 **Listen to a man describing a family member, then answer True or False to these questions:**

a The man is talking about his eldest daughter.

b The girl's name is Maria.

c She is 16.

d She is a secretary.

e She's sporty.

1 Match up the English and Portuguese.

a	This is my husband.	1	Este é o nosso filho.
b	That is my sister.	2	Sou elegante.
c	This is our son.	3	Tenho catorze anos.
d	That is my youngest sister.	4	Aquela é a minha irmã mais nova.
e	My teacher is serious.	5	Quantos anos tens?
f	I am elegant.	6	Aquela é a minha irmã.
g	How old are you?	7	O meu professor é sério.
h	I am fourteen.	8	Este é o meu marido.

2 For each sentence, decide if the choice of verb is correct. If it isn't, supply the right verb in its appropriate form:

   a Ela é com a família.
   b Eu estou sozinho.
   c John é nove anos.
   d Os filhos estão mais altos.
   e Nós temos uma casa moderna.
   f A minha irmã é honesta.

SELF CHECK

I CAN...
. . . point people out
. . . describe my family
. . . talk about age

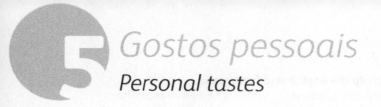

Gostos pessoais
Personal tastes

In this unit you will learn how to:
▶ *say what you like or dislike.*
▶ *say what you prefer.*
▶ *ask other people about their preferences.*

CEFR: (A2) *Can explain what he / she likes or dislikes about something;* **(A2)** *can use simple descriptive language to make brief statements about and compare objects and possessions.*

 Calling someone *you*

In this unit you will begin to find a mixture of forms of address (how to call someone you). Remember that, between friends and young people, the **tu** form is used, and with older people, and people who do not know each other very well, you will hear the polite forms of **o senhor / a senhora**, or **o / a** plus the person's name. Don't forget that the verb will often be used on its own, without a corresponding word for *you*. When talking to more than one person, you can either use the plurals **os senhores / as senhoras** or simply the plural form of the appropriate verb. You will see this demonstrated in the first dialogue. **Os senhores** can be used either to a group of men, or a mixed group or a couple.

What form would you use with a female stranger, to ask directions? What word would youngsters use with each other?

Diálogo

Fátima is finding out if the Green family likes Portuguese food.

1 05.01 **First of all, listen to the key expressions and try to repeat them.**

os senhores gostam ...?	*do you (pl) like ...?*
a comida portuguesa	*Portuguese food*
gostamos	*we (do) like*
muito	*a lot, very*
saudável	*healthy*
delicioso/a	*delicious*
mas	*but*
gosto mais	*I like more*
tipicamente	*typically*
um pouco	*a bit, a little*
claro	*of course*
imenso	*a great deal, a lot*

2 05.02 **Now listen to the dialogue and work out the answers to these questions: Does Mrs Green like sardines? Why / Why not?**

Fátima	Então, os senhores gostam da comida portuguesa?
Sr Green	Gostamos muito. A comida é saudável e muito deliciosa.
Fátima	Ótimo! A Senhora Green gosta de sardinhas?
Sra Green	Gosto, mas não muito. Têm muito sal. Gosto mais de frango.
Sr Green	Eu também gosto de frango. A nossa filha gosta muito de arroz de marisco.
Fátima	Não gostam do caldo verde? É tipicamente português.
Sra Green	Gostamos um pouco. E a Fátima, gosta da comida portuguesa?
Fátima	Claro, sou portuguesa, e os portugueses gostam imenso de comida!

3 **Can you work out the missing English words? These essential expressions all appear in the dialogue.**

gosta ...?	*do you (he, she) like ...?*
(as) sardinhas	_____
gosto	_____
têm	*they have*
(o) sal	_____
(o) frango	*chicken*

também	*also*
(o) arroz de marisco	*seafood rice*
não gostam ...?	*don't you like ...?*
(o) caldo verde	*shredded kale soup*
gostam	*they like*

Language discovery

1 MORE ON -AR VERBS

Gostar, like some of the verbs you learnt in Units 2 and 3 (**morar, trabalhar, falar**), is what is known as a regular verb, i.e. it follows a normal pattern of endings for that group of verbs. It belongs to the biggest verb group in Portuguese – those which end in **-ar**. With only a few exceptions, all these verbs are formed in the same way:

First you take off the **-ar** ending and you are left with what is called the stem.

Gostar – ar = **gost** (the stem)

Then you add on to this stem the appropriate ending according to whoever is doing the action.

For **-ar** verbs, the endings you require are as follows:

stem +	
-o	*I*
-as	*you (informal)*
-a	*he, she, it, you (polite)*
-amos	*we*
-am	*they, you (plural)*

Here are a few examples:

falo	*I speak*	**gostamos**	*we like*
moras	*you live*	**moram**	*they, you live*
trabalha	*he / she works / you work*		

The meanings are sometimes ambiguous, so to make sure you really know who is doing the action, you may need to use the words for *he* (**ele**), *she* (**ela**), or *they* (**eles, elas**).

Using the examples above and the rules for endings, how would you say: *he lives, I like, they* (fem) *work*?

The verb **gostar** is followed by the word **de**, when that precedes a noun (thing) or a verb.

Gosta *de* frango?	*Do you like chicken?*
Sim, gosto.	*Yes, I do (like it).*
Gosto *de* comer frango.	*I like to eat chicken.*

The word **de** (which really serves no function in the sentence – it's one of those 'oddments' mentioned earlier in the book), combines with the words **o / a / os / as**, to form **do, da, dos, das**.

Gosto *do* frango.	I like the chicken.
Gostamos *das* sardinhas.	We like the sardines.
Ela não gosta *da* comida.	She doesn't like the food.

You can describe just how much you do or do not like something by using words such as **muito** (*a lot, much*), **um pouco** (*a little bit*), **não muito** (*not much*), and **imenso** (*a great deal*). This last one is used a lot by Portuguese people.

In the Dialogue, what expression does Sr Green use to mean *we like it very much*? And how does Sra Green say: *I do, but not much*?

When the Portuguese want to convey the meaning of *yes, I do*, they simply repeat the verb in the right person:

Gostam da comida?	*Do you like the food?*
Gostamos, sim.	*Yes, we do (like it).*
Não, não gostamos.	*No, we don't (like it).*

Practice 1

1 How would you say the following?
   a Do Mr and Mrs Brito like chicken?
   b Don't you (informal) like the shredded kale soup?
   c No, I don't (like).
   d We like sardines a lot.
   e Paula likes seafood rice a little.
   f They like Portuguese food a great deal.

2 **Choose the correct endings for the verbs in the sentences below. Here are the endings: -o / -as / -a / -amos / -am.**
   a A Maria trabalh___ num hospital.
   b Eu (*I*) não gost___ do frango.
   c Nós (*we*) mor___ em Lisboa.
   d Tu não gost___ do caldo verde?
   e Os senhores fal___ inglês.

3 **Match up the questions on the left to the most likely answers on the right. Remember some verb forms can refer to different people.**
   a Tu gostas do arroz de marisco?   1 Gostamos um pouco.
   b Os senhores gostam da comida?   2 O Miguel gosta muito.
   c A Paula não gosta do frango?   3 Sim, gosto muito.
   d Quem (*who*) gosta das sardinhas?   4 Não, não gosta.
   e O seu filho não gosta do caldo verde?   5 Não, ela não gosta
                                                   muito.

4 **Língua viva – What is this restaurant advert inviting you to come and try?**

Listening and reading

Nuno talks about his family's preferences for different countries.

1 **Listen to some of the key expressions first.**

porque	*because*
um país	*a country*
caro	*expensive*
para nós	*for us*
pessoalmente	*personally*
prefiro	*I prefer*
agradável	*pleasant, enjoyable*
prefere	*she / he prefers / you prefer*
a comida dinamarquesa	*Danish food*
preferimos	*we prefer*
um lugar	*a place*
(o) barulho	*noise*

2 **Now read and listen to the passage carefully. Can you work out the reasons for their likes and dislikes?**

Bom, gostamos todos da Suíça, porque é um país muito limpo, mas é um pouco caro para nós. Pessoalmente, prefiro a Austrália, porque tem um clima agradável. A minha mulher prefere a Dinamarca, porque ela gosta imenso da comida dinamarquesa. Não gostamos muito do Japão porque é muito movimentado. Preferimos um lugar mais calmo, como a Holanda. Os nossos filhos preferem o barulho. Eles gostam imenso dos Estados Unidos.

3 **Can you guess the names of the four countries, all taken from the passage?**

a Suíça	_____
limpo	*clean*
um clima	*a climate*
a Dinamarca '	_____
o Japão	_____
movimentado	*busy, crowded*
calmo	*calm*
a Holanda	_____
preferem	*they / you prefer*

1 Choose the correct answer for each question.

   a A família do Nuno gosta da Suíça? Sim, gosta. / Não, não gosta.

   b Porquê? (*Why?*) Porque é um país muito sujo / limpo.

   c Porque é que o Nuno prefere a Austrália? Porque tem um clima agradável / comida deliciosa.

   d Eles gostam do Japão? Não, não gostam muito. / Sim, gostam muito.

   e Quem prefere a Dinamarca? Os filhos / a mulher do Nuno.

   f Porque é que os filhos preferem os Estados Unidos? Porque preferem o barulho / o clima.

Language discovery

1 DESCRIBING PLACES

In Unit 4 you learnt some words (adjectives) for describing people. In the Reading passage you were introduced to some words to use when describing places (towns, countries), such as **limpo**, **caro**, and **movimentado**.

You might also want to try out the following:

Can you guess what the meanings are in English of the missing words?

barulhento/a	noisy
sujo/a	dirty
aborrecido/a	boring
desagradável	_____
moderno/a	_____
antigo / velho/a	old
barato/a	cheap
bonito/a	nice, pretty (picturesque)
histórico/a	_____
interessante	_____
cultural	_____

When asking people about their preferences about various items, you can ask them **(o) que prefere?**

O que prefere – frango ou sardinhas?   *What do you prefer, chicken or sardines?*

You can also use **qual prefere?** (*Which do you prefer?*):

Qual prefere – o Japão ou a Holanda?   *Which do you prefer, Japan or Holland?*

Don't forget to make the verb plural (**preferem**) if you are talking to more than one person.

Que preferem – vinho ou cerveja?   *What do you prefer, wine or beer?*

Practice 3

1 **Form the adjectives correctly to match what each one is describing (masculine, feminine, singular or plural).**
   a O hotel é muito barulhent____.
   b As casas são modern____.
   c Esta cidade não é históric____.
   d A comida é barat____.
   e Os vinhos são interessante____.

2 **Complete the sentences according to the English prompts:**
   a (*I prefer*) _____ a Inglaterra porque é (*cultural*) _____.
   b (*We like*) _____ Portugal porque é (*pretty*) _____.
   c (*Do you,* plural, *like*) _____ (*Italian food*) _____?
   d (*I do not like*) _____ (*Japan*) _____; é muito movimentado.

3 **Língua viva – What kind of férias (*holidays*) is this advertisement inviting you to take this year?**

ESTE ANO
faça férias
diferentes!

4 Listen and practise answering questions about the foods and drinks you like. You will hear the answers following each prompt.

5 Complete the grid with ten words that describe places. Follow the cues to find five pairs of opposites.

  1 is not quiet.
  2 is unpleasant.
  3 is not clean.
  4 is inexpensive.
  5 is the opposite of 4.
  6 is the opposite of 2.
  7 is neither young nor recent.
  8 is the opposite of 1.
  9 is the opposite of 7
  10 is the opposite of 3.

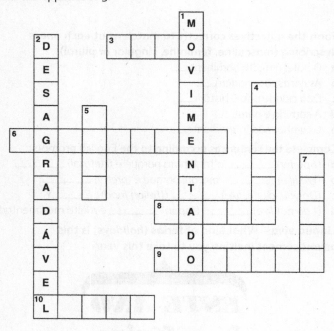

6 Form the verbs correctly. Choose from the box and supply the correct ending.

> pintar (to paint) cantar (to sing)
> limpar (to clean) conversar (to talk, chat)

  a he paints _____
  b we chat _____
  c I sing _____
  d Mary cleans _____ the house.
  e Do you (plural) sing? _____
  f you (singular, familiar) paint _____

Test yourself

1 To see what you have learnt in this unit, try saying the following:
  a Do you (singular, polite) like chicken?
  b I like sardines, a little.
  c Miguel likes Portuguese food a great deal.
  d Mr Green, don't you like the shredded kale soup?
  e I prefer Portugal because it's interesting.
  f Mr and Mrs Oliveira, which do you prefer: Italy or Japan?
  g We prefer Danish food.

2 Match the two halves of each sentence:

a Qual vinho prefere,	**1**	comida inglesa?
b Gosta da	**2**	um vinho tinto ou branco?
c Não gosto do	**3**	sopas portuguesas.
d Preferimos	**4**	cerveja ou vinho?
e Gostamos imenso das	**5**	vinho francês.
f Que preferem,	**6**	o frango.

6 Em casa
At home

In this unit you will learn how to:
▶ *describe your house.*
▶ *say where things are.*
▶ *say 'there is / there are'.*

CEFR: (A2) *Can describe everyday aspects of his / her environment, e.g. places;* **(A1)** *can get an idea of the content of simpler informational material and short simple descriptions, especially if there is visual support.*

 Houses

In Portuguese the word **casa** basically means *house*, although it encompasses the general idea of a residence. For example, you may hear people speaking about their **casa**, when, in fact, they live in **um apartamento** (*an apartment*). **Em casa** means *at home*, and the expressions **vou a casa** and **vou para casa** both mean *I'm going / I go home*.

If you are being shown around a house, you may hear the expressions **em cima** (*upstairs*) and **em baixo** (*downstairs*). The word for an individual *room*, or *living space*, is **assoalhada**. The ground floor is called **o rés-do-chão**, and in the lift you will see it abbreviated to r/c. All the other floors are simply numbered 1°, 2°, 3°, and so on. The ° is the last letter of the appropriate number: **primeiro** (*first*), **segundo** (*second*), and so on.

Many of the Portuguese words for the rooms around the house are similar to English ones, and if you stretch your imagination a little bit, you can make informed guesses.

 What do you think a **sala de estar** is? How about a **cozinha**? Or even a **garagem**?

Listening and reading 1

1 06.01 **Roberto is talking about where he lives. Listen first to the new key expressions.**

um edifício	*a building*
grande	*big*
há	*there is / there are*
há dois quartos	*there are two bedrooms*
é fácil de limpar	*it's easy to clean*
de vez em quando	*from time to time, sometimes*
não funciona	*it doesn't work*
a única coisa	*the only thing*
que	*which, that*

2 06.02 **Now read the passage as you listen. Does Roberto live in a house or an apartment?**

Moro em Lisboa, num apartamento moderno. Fica no quinto andar dum edifício muito alto. O apartamento não é muito grande. Há dois quartos, uma sala, uma cozinha e uma casa de banho. Gosto muito do apartamento porque é fácil de limpar. O edifício tem elevador mas, de vez em quando, não funciona. Esta é a única coisa de que não gosto!

3 Match the Portuguese and English house words, which all appear in the dialogue:

a	o quarto	**1**	the lift
b	a sala	**2**	a kitchen
c	uma cozinha	**3**	the bedroom
d	uma casa de banho	**4**	a bathroom
e	o elevador	**5**	the living room

Which sentence in the passage means *This is the only thing I don't like*? You might find it useful to learn expressions like this one as a complete sentence. It will make your Portuguese sound more fluent. Now how would you say *This is the only thing I like*?

 Diálogo

Ana Maria is talking to a friend about her house in the country town of Elvas.

 1 06.03 **You will hear the key expressions first. Listen and repeat, trying to imitate the speaker.**

como é a casa?	*what's the house like?*
o Bairro de Boa Vista	*the Boa Vista district, neighborhood*
típica (f) da região	*typical of the region*
quantas assoalhadas tem?	*how many rooms does it have?*
uma sala de jantar	*a dining room*
em cima	*upstairs*
com terraço	*with (a) balcony*

2 06.04 **Now listen to the dialogue and answer the questions.**

   a How many bedrooms are there?

Ana Maria	Gosto imenso da minha casa.
Júlia	Como é a casa?
Ana Maria	Bem, é bastante grande, e tem dois andares. Fica no Bairro de Boa Vista, e é típica da região.
Júlia	Quantas assoalhadas tem?
Ana Maria	Em baixo há uma sala de estar, e uma de jantar, e também uma cozinha grande.
Júlia	E em cima?
Ana Maria	Em cima há dois quartos pequenos e um quarto grande com terraço e uma casa de banho bonita.

   b How large is the house?
   c What rooms are there downstairs?
   d Does Ana Maria like the house?

Language discovery

1 HÁ *THERE IS, THERE ARE*

This little word is extremely versatile as you can use it to talk about something in either the singular or plural:

Há uma sala. *There is a lounge.*

Há dois quartos. *There are two bedrooms.*

It can be used as a question: *is there, are there?*

Há um jardim? *Is there a garden?*

Quantos quartos há na casa? *How many rooms are there in the house?*

And it is turned into the negative *there is not, there are not*, by placing the word **não** before it:

Não há uma casa de banho. *There isn't a bathroom.*

Practice 1

1 **Look at the sketch, and complete the paragraph to describe the house.**

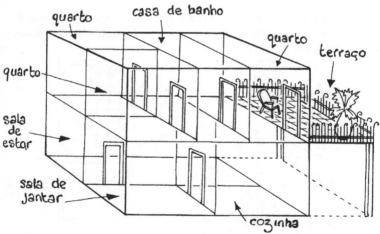

A casa da família Ferreira é antiga e _____ da região. Na casa há _____ quartos. Há dois _____ e um _____ com _____. Em cima também _____ uma _____ _____ _____. Em _____ há uma _____, uma sala _____ estar e uma _____ _____ _____.

2 How would you describe your own living space? Start with ... **a minha casa / o meu apartamento** ..., and choose words from each box to help you with the description. If you need some help, there's a typical answer in the Key to the exercises.

é	uma casa	}	antigo/a
			moderno/a
	um apartamento		típico/a da região

fica	num edifício	} antigo		rés-do-chão
	num bairro	moderno	**no**	primeiro
				segundo	} andar
				terceiro

	em cima	**em baixo**
na casa há	1,2,3 quartos	uma cozinha
	uma casa de banho	uma sala de jantar
	um terraço	uma sala de estar

Gosto / Não gosto da minha casa.

3 Look at the floor plan. Then see if you can describe the ground floor of this house by completing the paragraph with the words from the box.

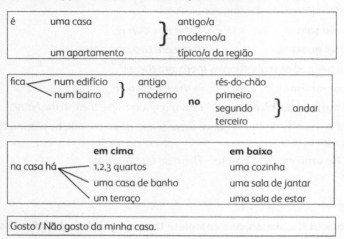

baixo   há   sala   grande   estar

Em **(a)** _____ há uma cozinha **(b)** _____. **(c)** _____ uma sala de **(d)** _____ e uma **(e)** _____ de jantar.

56

Listening and reading 2

In this 'through the keyhole' tour of Paula's house, she describes where various pieces of furniture are located.

1 06.05 **First of all, you will hear some new key expressions.**

primeiro	*first of all*	entre	*in between*
onde	*where*	a máquina de lavar	*washing machine*
em frente de	*in front of*	debaixo de	*underneath*
ao lado de	*next to*	a parede	*wall*
em cima de	*on top of*	detrás de	*behind*

2 06.06 **Now listen to, and read, the passage. What is the word for** *fridge*?

Primeiro, estamos na sala, onde há um sofá em frente da lareira, e ao lado do sofá, duas poltronas. Há um vaso de flores em cima da estante. Na cozinha há um fogão entre o frigorífico e a máquina de lavar. O meu gato está debaixo da mesa. No meu quarto há um quadro bonito na parede, e detrás da porta há um armário. Na casa de banho há um chuveiro.

3 Work out the missing English meaning of the words below, which are all found in the passage.

um sofá	_____	a mesa	*table*
a lareira	*fireplace*	um quadro	*a picture*
a poltrona	*armchair*	na (= em + a)	*on the*
um vaso de flores	_____	a porta	*door*
a estante	*bookcase*	um armário	_____
um fogão	*a cooker*	um chuveiro	*a shower*
o gato	_____		

4 06.07 **Can you answer these questions, in Portuguese, based on the Reading passage? Listen to the audio to confirm your answers.**

a Onde está o sofá?
b O que há (*what is there*) em cima da estante?
c Onde está o gato?
d Há uma mesa na cozinha?
e O que há no quarto da Paula?
f Há uma poltrona na casa de banho?

Go further

The Reading passage introduced you to some of the more common Portuguese expressions for describing where things (or people) are. These words are known as prepositions: the word position should help you to remember their function. Many Portuguese prepositions are made up of more than one word, and often end with the word **de**. Did you notice in the passage how the **de** combined, or contracted, with the words for *the* or *a*? You should now be becoming familiar with these contracted forms – they are very common in Portuguese. For example:

detrás da (= de + a) poltrona   *behind the chair*

debaixo duma (= de + uma) mesa   *under a table*

How would you say *on top of the table* and *in front of the sofa*?

You will meet more of these as you go along.

Don't forget when describing the location of items that can move, use the verb **estar** for *is* (**está**) and *are* (**estão**).

 Practice 2

1 **Look at the diagram of Jorge's sala de estar, and decide if the statements are V verdadeiro (*true*) or F falso (*false*).**

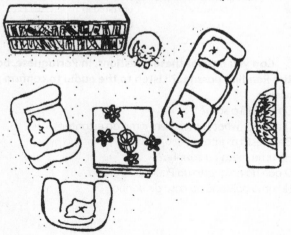

Na sala de estar:
  a Há três poltronas.
  b O gato está detrás da estante.
  c Há um vaso de flores debaixo da mesa.
  d Há um sofá em frente da lareira.
  e A estante está entre as poltronas.
  f Há uma poltrona ao lado da mesa.

2 **How would you say the following?**
  a The cat is on top of the fridge.
  b There is a cupboard next to the bookcase.
  c Is there a sofa behind the table?
  d The shower is not in the kitchen.
  e The cooker is next to the washing machine.
  f Is the cat in front of the armchair?

3 **Língua viva – How much of this advert in the classifieds can you understand?**
  a How many bedrooms are there in this advertised house?
  b Is there a fireplace in the living room?

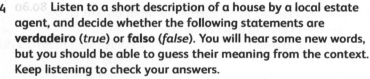

> # CASA DE CAMPO
> ## RIBATEJO
>
> Linda moradia, sala c/ lareira, 3 quartos, 2 wc,
> c/ quintal e garagem. Sossego e ar puro.
> **Tel. 793 54 40/88 – Sr. Ferreira**

The abbreviation **c/** means **com** (*with*).

4 06.08 **Listen to a short description of a house by a local estate agent, and decide whether the following statements are verdadeiro (*true*) or falso (*false*). You will hear some new words, but you should be able to guess their meaning from the context. Keep listening to check your answers.**
  a Casa Rosa is an old house.
  b It has a kitchen-diner.
  c There are kitchen appliances included in the price.
  d There are only two bedrooms.
  e The garage is big enough for two cars.

5 Earlier you heard Roberto describe his apartment. Listen once more if you need to remind yourself. He has now decided to rent it out and has advertised it on the Internet. Look at the floor plan and choose the appropriate words to complete the description.

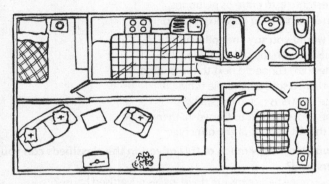

Aluga-se! For rent!

Apartamento moderno / velho em Lisboa / Braga. Fica no rés-do-chão / quinto andar dum edifício alto / típico da região. O edifício tem / não tem elevador. O apartamento tem dois / três quartos e uma sala de jantar / uma sala. Há cozinha / garagem e casa de banho.

6 A potential tenant wants further information. Match the questions in English and Portuguese.

a	Is it easy to clean?	**1**	O apartamento é muito grande?
b	Does the lift work?	**2**	O que há na sala?
c	Is the apartment very big?	**3**	É fácil de limpar?
d	What's the district like?	**4**	Como é o bairro?
e	What is there in the living room?	**5**	O elevador funciona?

1 How would you say the following?

a I have an apartment.
b My house has three bedrooms.
c What is your house like?
d I have a large kitchen.
e There are two bathrooms.
f There isn't a dining room.
g The sofa is next to the table.
h The fridge is in the kitchen.
i What is there in the living room?

2 Match up the questions and answers:

a O apartamento é grande?
b Quantas assoalhadas tem?
c Há um jardim?
d Gosta da sua casa?
e Onde está o gato?
f O que há em frente da estante?

1 Não, não há.
2 Há um sofa.
3 Sim, gosto muito.
4 Não, é pequeno.
5 Está debaixo da cama.
6 Tem sete.

SELF CHECK

I CAN...
. . . describe my house
. . . say where things are
. . . say 'there is' / 'there are'

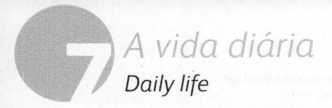

A vida diária
Daily life

In this unit you will learn how to:
▶ *talk about daily activities.*
▶ *name the days of the week.*
▶ *tell the times of the day.*
▶ *use numbers 21–100.*

CEFR: (A1) *Can handle numbers and time;* **(A2)** *can ask and answer questions about habits and routines.*

 Daily routine

A rotina diária (*daily routine*) in Portugal often starts with a quick **pequeno almoço** (*breakfast*), and for many Portuguese on the move early there follows a brief stop in a café for **uma bica** or **um café** (*an expresso*) and often a cake! The idea of packing a lunch for work is not typical; most people eat out in cafés and **tascas** (*cheap cafés*).

Small shops often close during part of the afternoon, typically anytime between 2 and 5 p.m., sometimes referred to as **a sesta** (*siesta* or *rest*), although the Portuguese are keen to insist they don't necessarily fall asleep at this point, contrary to the stereotypical image of their Spanish neighbours! Shops open again for when most people leave work, and stay open into the evening. **O jantar** (*dinner*) is not eaten as late as in Spain, most Portuguese dining mid-evening, and often walking out to **passear** (*have a stroll*) and **tomar um café ou um copo** (*have a coffee or a drink*) out in the streets rather than at home.

 Which do you think is the word for *lunch*?

07.01 You will now hear ten numbers you have met before. Do you recognize them?

What about working the other way round? What would these numbers be in Portuguese? 12   6   18   2   15   10

Practise until you can produce these numbers easily.

OS DIAS DA SEMANA *THE DAYS OF THE WEEK*

 07.02

a segunda-feira	*Monday*
a terça-feira	*Tuesday*
a quarta-feira	*Wednesday*
a quinta-feira	*Thursday*
a sexta-feira	*Friday*
o sábado	*Saturday*
o domingo	*Sunday*

Weekdays are 'numbered' from Monday through Friday as the 2nd to the 5th. In spoken Portuguese, it is usual to drop the word **feira**, and speak simply in terms of **a terça**, **a quinta**, etc. Having Monday as the 'second' day of the week harks back to early Christendom and its adoption of **sábado** (*Saturday*) as the 'sabbath' and **domingo** (*Sunday*) as the first day of the new week.

Listening and reading

 1 07.03 **Rosa is describing her daily routine. First of all, listen to the key expressions.**

levanto-me	*I get up*
tomo banho	*I have a bath*
visto-me	*I get dressed*
tomo o pequeno almoço	*I have breakfast*
saio para apanhar o autocarro	*I leave to catch the bus*
chego	*I arrive*
começo o trabalho	*I begin work*
almoço	*I have lunch*
janto	*I dine*
vou a uma aula de inglês	*I go to an English class*
deito-me	*I go to bed*

2 07.04 **Now, listen to and read the text, Then answer the questions.**

> Levanto-me às sete horas da manhã. Tomo banho e visto-me. Às sete e meia tomo o pequeno almoço, e saio para apanhar o autocarro às oito horas. Chego ao escritório às oito e vinte, e começo o trabalho às oito e meia. Ao meio-dia almoço. Saio do trabalho às cinco e um quarto e chego a casa às seis horas da tarde. Janto por volta das sete, e às quartas-feiras à noite vou a uma aula de inglês. Deito-me às dez menos um quarto.

Like • Comment • Share

a What is the third activity Rosa lists?
b What activity is mentioned just prior to arriving home?
c What does she do on Wednesday evenings?

 Using what you know, how would you say *I arrive at the office*?

3 07.05 **Listen to the times Rosa mentioned for her daily activities. Repeat each one, then, looking only at the English, try to remember how to say the time.**

às sete horas da manhã	*at seven in the morning*
às sete e meia	*at half past seven*
às oito horas	*at eight o'clock*
às oito e vinte	*at twenty past eight*
às oito e meia	*at half past eight*
ao meio-dia	*at noon, midday*
às cinco e um quarto	*at quarter past five*
às seis horas da tarde	*at six in the evening*
por volta das sete	*around seven*
às quartas-feiras à noite	*on Wednesday evenings*
às dez menos um quarto	*at quarter to ten*

4 **Read Rosa's daily routine once more. Then match the following activities and times.**

a	levanto-me	**1**	08.00
b	saio para apanhar o autocarro	**2**	21.45
c	deito-me	**3**	12.00
d	começo o trabalho	**4**	07.00
e	almoço	**5**	08.30

Language discovery

1 TWO IRREGULAR VERBS

Most of the verbs listed as Rosa's activities fall into the regular group of **-ar** verbs, the formation of which you learnt in Unit 5. Therefore, *she arrives* will be **chega**, *we begin* will be **começamos**, and *they dine* will be **jantam**. Have a quick look back at Unit 5, if you cannot remember the various verb endings.

Saio, and **vou**, belong to verb groups which follow different patterns for many of their endings.

sair *to go out*		ir *to go*	
(eu) saio	*I go out*	**(eu) vou**	*I go*
(tu) sais	*you go out*	**(tu) vais**	*you go*
(ele/ela, o sr, etc.) sai	*he / she / it / you go(es) out*	**(ele/ela, o sr, etc.) vai**	*he / she / it / you go(es)*
(nós) saímos	*we go out*	**(nós) vamos**	*we go*
(eles, elas, os srs, etc.) saem	*they / you (pl) go out*	**(eles, elas, os srs etc.) vão**	*they / you go*

2 LEVANTO-ME *I GET DRESSED*

You will have noticed some of the verbs describing Rosa's activities had a **-me** joined on to them. Remember also, that you met this kind of verb in Unit 1, when giving your name (**chamo-me**). The **-me** actually means *'myself'*, and so the literal meanings of these verbs are – *I get myself up, I call myself, I get myself dressed*, and so on. When you want to talk about other people doing these actions, there are different 'self' words. Here is the verb to get up with all the appropriate end-words.

(eu)	**levanto-me**	*I get up*
(tu)	**levantas-te**	*you get up*
(ele, ela, o sr, etc.)	**levanta-se**	*he / she / + you (polite) get(s) up*
(nós)	**levantamo-nos**	*we get up*
(eles, elas, os srs, etc)	**levantam-se**	*they / + you (plural) get up*

Be careful with the **nós** we form because it loses the final **-s** from the verb ending.

Use the information from Rosa's daily routine to answer this question: How would you say *she goes to bed*?

The Portuguese talk about time in terms of **as horas** *(the hours)*.

A que horas ... ?   *At what time ... ?*

Time on the hour is expressed as follows:

às + the number of +   **horas** *(optional)* + **da manhã** *(in the morning)*
        the hour

at   *(o clock)*   **da tarde** *(in the afternoon,*
                                                    evening)

                                               da noite *(at night)*

às   **sete**   **(horas)**   **da**   **manhã**   *at 7 a.m.*

às   **nove**   **(horas)**   **da**   **noite**   *at 9 p.m.*

ao meio-dia   *at midday*

à meia-noite   *at midnight*

à uma hora   *at one o'clock*

Time past the hour is expressed thus:

às   +   the hour   +   **e** *(and)*   **um quarto** *(a quarter)*
                                                 meia *(half)*
                                                 ... minutos *(minutes)*

às cinco (horas) e vinte (minutos)   *at 5.20*

às três e um quarto   *at 3.15*

às oito e meia   *at 8.30*

Again, you may want to specify whether you mean morning, afternoon or evening.

Time to the hour is expressed in a couple of ways. Here is one of them:

às   +   next full hour   +   **menos** *(less)*   +   **...minutos / um quarto**

às dez menos vinte   *at 9.40*

às oito menos um quarto   *at 7.45*

 07.06 **Listen to some times on the audio and try to work out what they are.**

To deal more effectively with time, you need numbers up to 60 at least, and as numbers are a part of our everyday lives, here is the next set for you to start learning.

21	**vinte e um/uma**	50	**cinquenta**
22	**vinte e dois/duas**	60	**sessenta**
23	**vinte e três**	70	**setenta**
24	**vinte e quatro**	80	**oitenta**
25	**vinte e cinco**	90	**noventa**
30	**trinta**	100	**cem (cento)**
40	**quarenta**		

Can you see the pattern of formation? You simply use the word **e** (*and*) to join the two lots of digits together. Don't forget, wherever one, or two occur, you must decide to use either the masculine or feminine form. e.g. **vinte e duas mesas**, *22 tables*. There are two forms for 100: **cem** is used for a round one hundred, and **cento** for any combination over a hundred (101, 125, and so on).

How would you say: *He's 21 years old?*

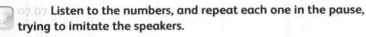

07.07 **Listen to the numbers, and repeat each one in the pause, trying to imitate the speakers.**

Practice 1

1 07.08 **Listen and say what you think each number is.**

2 **Look at Maurício's diary entry for quarta-feira (*Wednesday*), and complete the statements about his daily activities.**

Quarta-feira			
7.15 a.m.	**levanto-me**	5.20 p.m.	**saio do**
8.30 a.m.	**saio**		**trabalho**
9.00 a.m.	**começo o**	6.45 p.m.	**janto**
	trabalho	7.40 p.m.	**aula de japonês**
1.00 p.m.	**almoço**	11.25 p.m.	**deito-me**

O Maurício _____ às 7.15.
b Começa o trabalho às _____.
c Ele _____ às ___ menos _____ _____.
d Às 7.40 tem uma _____ _____ _____.
e O Maurício almoça _____ _____.

3 The numbers below represent the house numbers on the doors. Can you match them up correctly?

a vinte e sete   **b** setenta e sete   **c** noventa e três

d trinta e cinco   **e** quarenta e um   **f** noventa e seis

1

35

2

96

3

27

4

93

5

41

6

77

4 Can you answer the following questions about your own daily routines? Check in the Key to the exercises if you need help.

a What time do you get up?
b What time do you have lunch?
c What time do you arrive home?
d What time do you go to bed?

5 Match the clock times to the statements about the daily activities that various people do.

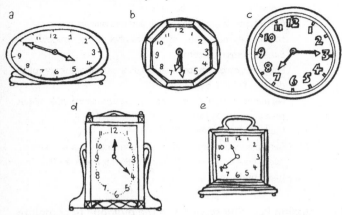

a
b
c
d
e

1 A Maria levanta-se às seis e meia.
2 Jorge almoça ao meio-dia e vinte.
3 O Manuel sai do trabalho às cinco menos dez.
4 A Lídia janta às sete e um quarto.
5 O Filipe chega ao trabalho às onze menos vinte.

Diálogo 1

1 07.09 **Rui and João are talking about their weekend routines. Listen to some key expressions first.**

aos sábados	on Saturdays
geralmente / em geral	generally
mais tarde	later
depois	then, after
para passear	(in order) to stroll around
aos domingos	on Sundays
cedo	early
parte	departs, leaves
igreja	church
o resto do dia	the rest of the day

2 07.10 **Now listen to the conversation. How do you say** *we dine*?

Rui	A que horas se levanta aos sábados?
João	Geralmente às oito e meia. Eu e a minha mulher vamos às compras, e o nosso filho vai jogar futebol com os amigos.
Rui	E a que horas almoçam?
João	Em geral não comemos muito ao almoço. Jantamos por volta das sete horas. E o Rui?
Rui	Na minha casa também jantamos mais tarde, e depois saímos para passear na praça.
João	O que faz aos domingos?
Rui	Bem, a minha mulher levanta-se e come cedo, e parte para a igreja. Passamos o resto do dia em família, e não nos deitamos muito tarde.

3 **Find the missing Portuguese words in the dialogue to complete these expressions, which are all extra useful vocabulary.**

vamos às compras	*we go shopping*
(os) amigos	*friends*
vai _____ futebol	*he goes to play football*
comemos	*we eat*
(a) praça	*town square*
_____	*she eats*
passamos	*we spend*
em família	*together, as a family*

4 **Now answer these questions about the two friends' weekend routine.**

   a What time does João usually get up on Saturdays?
   b What does his son do with his friends?
   c Where does Rui's wife go on Sundays?

Language discovery

You may have noticed the changed position of the 'self' word **-se**, in this question. In Rosa's earlier description she said **levanto-me**. Whenever you have one of these verbs, known as reflexives, in a question, the reflexive bit of it (the 'self' word) is placed before the verb.

Can you remember how to ask *what's your name*, in this way?

2 NÃO NOS DEITAMOS TARDE *WE DON'T GO TO BED LATE*

This is another example where the reflexives change their position and go in front of the verb – wherever a negative is used. So you could have:

Levanta-se cedo. *He gets up early.*

but

Não se levanta tarde. *He doesn't get up late.*

3 -ER AND -IR VERB GROUPS

Up to now you have worked with **-ar** verbs, and a few irregular verbs. There are two other main verb groups, examples of which you saw in the dialogue. They are the **-er** and **-ir** groups.

comer *to eat*		partir *to depart / leave*	
eu	como	eu	parto
tu	comes	tu	partes
ele, ela, *you*	come	ele, ela, *you*	parte
nós	comemos	nós	partimos
eles, elas, *you* (pl)	comem	eles, elas, *you* (pl)	partem

Can you see the similarities between the two? Earlier, you had the verb **visto-me** (*I get dressed*). This belongs to the **-ir** group (**vestir**), but the *I* person is slightly different.

What difference can you see between **comer** and **partir** in the table?

Like previous contracted forms, the preposition **a** (*to, at*), which should not be confused with the feminine word for '*the*' (but often is!), combines with the words for *the*, to form the following:

ao = a + o   aos = a + os   à = a + a   às = a + as

ao trabalho   *to (the) work*   **à igreja**   *to (the) church*

aos escritórios   *to the offices*   **às casas**   *to the houses*

 Practice 2

1   Língua viva – When can you not visit this establishment?

cervejaria
XANA

PETISCOS
CARACÓIS
PÃO COM CHOURIÇO

Aberto das 7:30 às 22:00h.
Encerra à 4° feira, de manhã.

Bairro da Malagueira
Rua da Conduta, 16
Tel. 735862

2   How would you say the following?
  a I get up early.
  b He does not go to bed late.
  c What time do you (pl) get dressed?
  d We do not get dressed quickly (**rapidamente**).
  e What are they called?
  f What time do you (informal) get up?

3 Complete these sentences by choosing the correct verb form from the box. (You'll only need half the words). The appropriate verb is given to you on each line.

parte   come   vivem   compreende   abres   bebe   partes
partes   vivemos   compreendo   comemos   abro   bebemos

a Ele _____ (compreender *understand*)
b A senhora _____ (partir *depart*)
c Nós _____ (comer *eat*)
d Os senhores _____ (viver *live*)
e Tu _____ (abrir *open*)
f O senhor Smith _____ (beber *drink*)

4 Supply the correct form of 'to / to the' in these sentences:
a A Maria vai _____ hospital.
b O Miguel oferece um presente _____ senhoras.
c Vamos _____ Lisboa.
d Eles vão _____ escola.
e Vou _____ Londres.
f Tu vais _____ museus em Paris ?

Diálogo 2

Senhor Buisel has to get to the airport on time. He asks his neighbour what time it is.

1 07.11 **Listen to the key expressions first.**

sabe que horas são?	*do you know what time it is?*
preciso de ...	*I need ...*
(o) aeroporto	*airport*
até breve	*see you soon*

2 07.12 **Now listen to the dialogue. What time is it?**

Sr Buisel	Bom dia, Dona Ana Maria.
Da Ana Maria	Bom dia, senhor Buisel.
Sr Buisel	Desculpe, mas a senhora sabe que horas são?
Da Ana Maria	São duas menos cinco.
Sr Buisel	Obrigado. Preciso de ir ao aeroporto. Até breve.

Go further

As with the time of day, earlier in this unit, asking and telling the time uses the word **horas**, and literally asks *what hours are they?* The answer follows the form: **são x horas** (or **é**, with one o'clock, midday and midnight). All the other times to and from the hour are the same as those you learnt earlier.

São três horas.	*It's 3 o'clock.*
São cinco menos vinte.	*It's twenty to five.*
É meia-noite e um quarto.	*It's quarter past midnight.*

 1 07.13 **Listen to some more time phrases, and work out what each expression is.**

24 HORAS *24 HOURS*

The 24-hour clock is not difficult to deal with if you know your numbers to 60 with confidence. The times given on the 24-hour clock, which you will invariably meet when asking about travel times, are simply two sets of numbers joined by **e** (*and*):

15.35	**quinze e trinta e cinco**
20.56	**vinte e cinquenta e seis**
07.15	**sete e quinze**

The conventions for a quarter and half are not used.

07.14 **Now listen to some examples and try to work them out.**

DONA

Senhor Buisel called his neighbour **Dona Ana Maria**. The word **Dona** is used as a sign of respect when talking to older ladies, whether they are married or not. You may also hear **a senhora Dona Ana Maria**. Both of these forms of address can be used with verbs to convey the polite form of you.

A Dona Patrícia está boa?	*Are you well (Dona Patrícia)?*

Portuguese forms of address are extremely varied, as you keep finding out. Remember to take your cues from the people around you, and, when in doubt, err on the polite side.

Test yourself

1 **How would you do the following?**

a Ask someone what time they get up.

b Say that we do not go to bed until (**até**) 10.30 p.m.

c Ask Paulo what time he has lunch on Sundays.

d Say that you do not eat much on Tuesdays.

e Ask Jorge what time he goes to church.

f Ask someone what time it is.

2 **Complete these sequences of numbers by supplying the correct Portuguese number in full:**

a 21	22	23	_____
b 60	_____	80	90
c 100	95	_____	85
d 32	42	52	_____
e 98	99	100	_____

3 **Ronaldo's daily routine is all jumbled up! Put the activities in the correct order:**

a _____ Às oito horas toma o pequeno almoço.

b _____ Janta em casa às oito horas da tarde.

c _____ Ronaldo levanta-se às sete e meia.

d _____ Deita-se tarde.

e _____ Veste-se às oito menos um quarto.

f _____ À uma e um quarto ele almoça com os amigos.

SELF CHECK

I CAN. . .
. . . talk about daily activities
. . . name the days of the week
. . . tell the times of the day
. . . use numbers 21–100

O tempo livre
Free time

In this unit you will learn how to:
▶ *talk about activities you enjoy.*
▶ *ask people what they like doing in their free time.*
▶ *use four very irregular verbs: listen, read, see and do.*

CEFR: (A2) *Can ask and answer questions about what they do (at work and) in free time; **(A2)** can communicate in simple and routine tasks requiring a simple and direct exchange of information on familiar and routine matters to do with (work and) free time.*

Leisure activities

The Portuguese enjoy a range of activities in their **tempo de lazer** (*leisure time*). Many delight in the cornucopia of **eventos musicais** (*musical events*) on offer across the country, from **música clássica** (*classical music*) to **concertos e espetáculos** (*concerts and shows*) of **ópera** (*opera*), jazz, and the traditional **ranchos folclóricos** (*folklore groups*) which sing and dance in most regions of Portugal. **O teatro** (*theatre*) is also very popular, especially in Lisbon and Porto.

Many people take advantage of Portugal's **áreas de beleza natural** (*areas of natural beauty*) and its huge coastline to indulge in outdoor pursuits, such as **nadar** (*swimming*), **mergulhar** (*diving*), **pescar** (*fishing*), **andar** (*walking*), or simply **ir à praia** (*going to the beach*).

Traditional activities, such as **costurar** (*sewing*), **fazer renda** (*lace-making*), and **jogar cartas** (*playing cards*) are as popular as ever with older generations, whilst the younger Portuguese are as techno-savvy as they come, with their **videojogos** (*video games*), **redes sociais** (*social networks*), and **telemóveis** (*mobile phones*).

Using the information above, can you work out how to say *jazz music*? How would you say: *I like the theatre*?

Diálogo

Some market research is being carried out in the street to find out what people like doing in their free time.

1 08.01 **Listen to the key expressions first.**

posso ... ?	*may I ... ?*
claro	*of course*
o que quer saber?	*what do you want to know?*
o que é que vocês gostam de fazer?	*what do you (pl) like to do?*
no tempo livre	*in your free time*
ora bem	*well*
a piscina	*swimming pool*
e você?	*and you?*
o que gosta de fazer?	*what do you like doing?*
as telenovelas brasileiras	*Brazilian soap operas*

2 08.02 **Now read along as you listen to the dialogue between the interviewer and three passers-by. Then answer the questions. You may choose to do Exercise 3 before answering the questions.**

a How do you say: *I love*, or *adore*?

Entrevistador	Boa tarde. Com licença, posso fazer uma pergunta?
Laura	Claro. O que quer saber?
Entrevistador	O que é que vocês gostam de fazer no tempo livre?
Laura	Ora bem. No meu tempo livre gosto de ouvir música clássica, e de pintar.
José	Eu gosto de ir à piscina, ou de vez em quando gosto de passear no campo.
Entrevistador	E você? O que gosta de fazer no seu tempo de lazer?
Ana	Pois, gosto muito de ler, e de ver televisão.
Entrevistador	E o que gosta de ver?
Ana	Adoro as telenovelas brasileiras.
Entrevistador	Ótimo!

b Who prefers participating in more physical activities?

c What type of TV programme does Ana enjoy?

d How would you say 'I love listening to music'?

3 Read the dialogue again and find the missing Portuguese words to complete the expressions.

fazer uma _____	to ask a question
no seu tempo de lazer	in your free / leisure time
ouvir _____	to listen to music
_____	to paint
_____ no campo	to walk in the countryside
ler	to read
_____	to watch (see)
a televisão	television

Language discovery

1 VOCÊ, VOCÊS YOU

Did you notice that the interviewer spoke with a different accent? That's because he was Brazilian. He also used a different form of address from the ones you have already met. **Você**, and the plural **vocês**, is how Brazilians say *you*. You will also hear these forms of address in Portugal, but they are less formal than the ones you have so far learnt. The verb forms are the same, whether you use **você** or **o senhor / a senhora**:

Você gosta de ler? *Do you like reading?*

O senhor gosta de ouvir música? *Do you enjoy listening to music, Sir?*

And in the plural:

Vocês gostam de pescar? *Do you like fishing?*

As senhoras gostam de fazer renda? *Do you ladies enjoy lace-making?*

2 POSSO? MAY / CAN I?

The usual response if someone asks **posso?** is **pode** (*you can*) or **sim, pode** (*yes, you can*) or even **claro que pode** (*of course you can*). The whole verb, in the present tense is as follows:

poder *to be able to (can)*			
eu posso	*I can*	**nós podemos**	*we can*
tu podes	*you (familiar) can*	**vocês podem**	*you (plural) can*
ele / ela pode	*he / she (it) can*	**eles / elas podem**	*they can*
você / o senhor / a senhora pode	*you can*	**vocês / os senhores / as senhoras podem**	*you (polite, plural) can*

3 O QUE É QUE GOSTA DE FAZER? *WHAT IS IT THAT YOU LIKE TO DO (LIKE DOING)?*

You should remember that in Unit 5, the verb **gostar de** (*to like*) was used with various nouns (things) to describe what you do or don't like. Now you can use the same verb to talk about activities you like doing, and as **gostar** is a straightforward **-ar** verb, you can also talk about other people's likes without too many problems.

O Nuno gosta de pintar.	*Nuno likes painting (to paint).*
Gostamos de ouvir música.	*We like listening to music.*

How would you say: *they like reading?*

Look at these two questions, both of which you heard in the dialogue:

O que é que gosta de fazer?

O que gosta de fazer?

Do you think their meaning is the same, or different?

Practice 1

1 See if you can do the following:

  a Ask Maria what she likes doing in her free time.

  b Say that you like diving.

  c Ask the da Silvas if they like travelling (**viajar**).

  d Ask José and Nuno if they like playing sports (**praticar desportos**).

  e Say that you don't like working in the garden.

  f Ask someone you know very well if they like swimming in their free time.

2 A Portuguese interviewer asks you what you and you family enjoy doing in your free time. Follow the prompts and complete the conversation.

Entrevistadora	Bom dia. Com licença, posso fazer umas perguntas?
You	**(a)** *Say yes, of course you can.*
Entrevistadora	São portugueses?
You	**(b)** *No, you're not Portuguese. You're all English. Tell her what city you're from.*
Entrevistadora	Mas fala português?
You	**(c)** *Say yes, you speak some Portuguese.*
Entrevistadora	Muito bem. Então, o que é que gosta de fazer no tempo livre?
You	**(d)** *Say that you like going to the theatre.*
Entrevistadora	E a sua família?
You	**(e)** *Say that your husband / wife likes to work in the garden, and that your children like playing sports.*
Entrevistadora	E vocês gostam de visitar Portugal?
You	**(f)** *Say, of course!*

3 08.03 **Now listen and confirm your answers.**

4 Língua viva – Study these two adverts. Which establishment would you visit if you liked artistic pursuits?

Casa do Brasil
CENTRO DE LÍNGUA, ARTE E CULTURA

Centro desportivo
João Pessoa

ténis futebol
natação em piscina olímpica

What sport do you think **natação** is?

Listening and reading

Sónia writes a blog about the activities she enjoys doing, and how often she does them.

1 08.04 **You will hear the key expressions first; repeat and practise your pronunciation with the speaker.**

às vezes	*sometimes*
ouço	*I listen to*
aos fins de semana	*at the weekend(s)*
passo tempo a ler	*I spend time reading*
leio	*I read*
as revistas e os jornais	*magazines and newspapers*
os livros românticos	*romantic books*
muitas vezes	*often, many times*
a biblioteca	*the library*

2 08.05 **Now read along as you listen. What type of music does Sónia prefer?**

> Gosto muito de ouvir música. Às vezes ouço a música rock mas geralmente prefiro a música jazz. Aos fins de semana passo muito tempo a ler. Leio revistas e jornais, e gosto de livros românticos. Vou muitas vezes à biblioteca para ler.

3 08.06 **Now find out what Nuno gets up to, and when. Listen to the key expressions first.**

jogar ténis	*to play tennis*
todos os dias	*each, every day*
tento	*I try*
pelo menos	*at least*
navegar na Internet	*to surf the Web*
todas as noites	*every night*
vejo	*I watch, see*
o meu programa preferido	*my favourite programme*
Quem quer ser milionário?	*Who wants to be a Millionaire?*

4 08.07 **Now read, and listen to the text. How often does Nuno play tennis?**

> Gosto imenso de praticar desportos. Adoro jogar ténis, e todos os dias tento jogar pelo menos uma hora. Também gosto de navegar na Internet, e todas as noites vejo a televisão. O meu programa preferido é 'Quem quer ser milionário'?

5 **Look at the two blogs again and answer these questions.**
   a What does Sónia do a lot of at weekends?
   b How often does she go to the library?
   c What two indoor activities does Nuno enjoy?
   d Who does more physical activity, Sónia or Nuno?

Language discovery

1 SOMETIMES, OFTEN, NEVER

There are many words to describe how frequently people do activities; some appeared in the blogs you have read: **às vezes**, **muitas vezes**, **todos os dias**, **todas as noites**.

 08.08 Here are some further suggestions:

nunca	*never*
de vez em quando	*sometimes*
uma vez por (semana)	*once a (week)*
cada (mês)	*each (month)*
todos os anos	*every year*
poucas vezes	*few times, very little*

In general, these expressions go before the verb,

Nunca vou ao cinema.   *I never go to the cinema.*

although some will fit naturally at the end of a sentence.

Vejo a televisão todos os dias.   *I watch television every day.*

Another everyday expression for watching TV is **assistir a televisão**.

2 OUÇO, LEIO, VEJO, FAÇO *I LISTEN, READ, SEE, DO (MAKE)*

The verbs **ouvir**, **ler**, **ver**, and **fazer** are all irregular in some way or other. Here are the four verbs in full:

	ouvir – to listen / hear	ler – to read	ver – to watch / see	fazer – to do / make
eu	**ouço**	**leio**	**vejo**	**faço**
tu	**ouves**	**lês**	**vês**	**fazes**
ele / ela (+it)	**ouve**	**lê**	**vê**	**faz**
você / o senhor / a senhora	**ouve**	**lê**	**vê**	**faz**
nós	**ouvimos**	**lemos**	**vemos**	**fazemos**
eles / elas	**ouvem**	**leem**	**veem**	**fazem**
vocês, os senhores / as senhoras	**ouvem**	**leem**	**veem**	**fazem**

3 PARA *IN ORDER TO*

Sónia said she goes to the library **para ler** (*to read*), and you may have wondered why you needed the word **para**, when in fact **ler** already means *to read*. This also arose in the last unit, when Rosa said she leaves her house **para apanhar o autocarro** (*to catch the bus*). In fact you need to use the word **para** (*in order to*) before any verb, when it is your intention or objective to do something.

Vou à cidade para fazer as compras.	*I go / am going to town (in order) to do the shopping.*

Practice 2

1 Complete the text, choosing from the words in the box.

> ouve   nunca   gosta   leio   vão   livros   joga   abro   dias
> lê   vejo   todas   vez   quando   fazem

Eu gosto de ler _____ de aventura. _____ todos os _____,
e também _____ a televisão. O meu marido _____ música clássica,
e _____ golfe. Ele _____ _____ o jornal, mas _____ de ler
revistas. As minhas filhas _____ à discoteca _____ as semanas, e de
_____ em _____ _____ renda com a avó (*grandmother*).

2 Link up the statements on the left with the verbs on the right, using **para** (*in order to*) to make complete sentences.

a   Vou à biblioteca   **1** fazer as compras.

b   Paula vai ao escritório   **2** dançar.

c   Vamos ao centro desportivo   **3** ler os livros.

d   Ela vai ao supermercado   **4** jogar ténis.

e   Eles vão à piscina   **5** nadar.

f   Mónica vai à discoteca   **6** trabalhar.

3 Complete the sentences with the correct forms of the verbs:

a   Eu _____ (ouvir) música todos os dias.

b   Tu não _____ (ler) muito.

c   O Marcelo _____ (ver) muitos filmes.

d   Nós não _____ (fazer) muitas atividades aos domingos.

e   Elas gostam de _____ (ouvir) ópera ao teatro.

4 **Língua viva** – Study this sign: How often is this restaurant open?

RESTAURANTE - BAR
2 IRMÃOS
ABERTO TODOS OS DIAS

Especialidades da Casa: CATAPLANA - BIFE À CASA - ENTRECOSTO
COZINHA TRADICIONAL PORTUGUESA - ALMOÇOS - JANTARES
_____ AR CONDICIONADO

SANTA EULÁLIA — TELEFONE: 54852 _____ 8200 ALBUFEIRA

5 08 09 Listen to Gabriela talking about her free time, then complete these statements by choosing the most appropriate word.

1 Gabriela likes to listen to _____ music.
   a classical   **b** rock   **c** Brazilian

2 She loves going to the _____.
   a theatre   **b** opera   **c** cinema

3 She goes swimming _____.
   a once a month   **b** once a week   **c** every day

4 She never _____.
   a watches TV   **b** reads   **c** does sewing

1 See if you can do the following:

 a Ask someone what they like to do in their free time.

 b Say what you like doing.

 c Respond to someone who has asked if they can take a chair from your table.

 d Say how often you watch television.

 e Ask Mr and Mrs da Costa if they often listen to music.

 f Say you're going to town to go shopping.

2 Match up the English and Portuguese time expressions.

a	todos os dias	**1**	very little
b	duas vezes por mês	**2**	each week
c	nunca	**3**	every day
d	poucas vezes	**4**	never
e	de vez em quando	**5**	sometimes
f	cada semana	**6**	twice a month

SELF CHECK

I CAN...
○ ... talk about activities I enjoy
○ ... ask people what they like doing in their free time
○ ... use four very irregular verbs: 'listen', 'read', 'see' and 'do'

As férias
Holidays

In this unit you will learn how to:
▶ *talk about holidays.*
▶ *use numbers 101–99.*
▶ *say the months of the year.*
▶ *talk about wanting to do things.*
▶ *talk about events in the future.*

CEFR: (A1) *Can indicate time by such phrases as next week; in November;* **(A2)** *can describe plans and arrangements, habits and routines.*

A people on the move

The Portuguese, especially those who come from **o campo** (*rural areas*), are very attached to their home towns. Throughout history, **a terra** (*the land*) has played an important part in the lives of the Portuguese, as Portugal has always been a predominantly agricultural country. It is not surprising, then, that the Portuguese refer to their home towns as **a minha terra** (*my land*). Nevertheless, they do like to **viajar** (*travel*), and end up settling all over the world. At the last count more than 6 million Portuguese emigrants were scattered around the globe. However, when it's time to **tirar férias** (*have a holiday*), they often prefer to stay on home soil, and who could blame them, with hundreds of kilometres of sandy **litoral** (*coastline*) to choose from, or the tranquil shade offered in **parques nacionais** (*national parks*)? **As férias ao estrangeiro** (*holidays abroad*) tend to take in other European countries, where families can often visit relatives who have emigrated. But, despite their globetrotting, it is often to **a terra** that their feet turn when they feel **saudades**, a distinctly Portuguese feeling of deep yearning for far-off places or people.

Using the information above, how would you say: *I like to have holidays abroad*?
What does it mean if someone is described as **não é da terra**?

Diálogo 1

Fernando is talking to a colleague, Júlio, about where he and his family usually spend their holidays.

1 09.01 **First of all, listen to the key expressions.**

tirar férias	*to take / have a holiday*
quer	*wants*
conhecer	*to get to know*
viajamos pela Europa	*we travel through / around Europe*
vários	*various*
o país	*country*
sempre	*always*
provar	*to try, taste*
as comidas estrangeiras	*foreign food*
o verão	*summer*

2 09.02 **Now listen to the dialogue and answer the questions.**

a Where is Júlio going on holiday?

Fernando	Então, Júlio, vai tirar férias este ano?
Júlio	Vou, sim. Vou para a Grécia. A minha mulher quer conhecer a cultura grega. E o Fernando? Onde vai?
Fernando	Geralmente, viajamos pela Europa, e ficamos em vários países. Sempre gostamos de provar as comidas estrangeiras. E os seus filhos, Júlio? Vão com vocês?
Júlio	Não. A minha filha nunca passa as férias connosco. Sempre vai com o namorado para a França. De vez em quando o nosso filho quer vir connosco, mas em geral prefere passar o verão na praia.

b What do Fernando and his family like to try abroad?
c Are Julio's children going with him?

3 Look back at the dialogue or use your intuition to supply the missing key words from the conversation.

a Grécia	
a cultura grega	Greek _____
o namorado	boyfriend
a namorada	girlfriend
a _____	France
vir	to come

Language discovery

1 TWO IRREGULAR VERBS: QUERER (TO WANT) AND VIR (TO COME)

	querer to want	vir to come
I	quero	venho
you (informal)	queres	vens
he / she / it / you	quer	vem
we	queremos	vimos
they / you (pl)	querem	vêm

2 TWO VERBS MEANING TO KNOW: SABER AND CONHECER

Both of these verbs mean *to know*. **Saber** is used to know a fact, or how to do something. **Conhecer** means to know a person or place, and to get to know someone or somewhere. You would say:

Sabe que horas são?   *Do you know what time it is?*

Não sei.   *I don't know.*

but

Não conheço a Áustria.   *I don't know Austria.*

Note: In the first person (*I* form) of **conhecer**, there is a spelling change; the **c** acquires a little tail (a **cedilha**) to maintain a soft-c sound.

3 POR

Can you work out what these expressions mean?
pelo mar   **pelas ruas**

The preposition **por** (with its main meanings of *through, by, along*)
combines with the words for *the* (**o, a, os, as**), and contracts into the
following forms **pelo, pela, pelos, pelas**.

Did you work out what **pela Europa** meant in the dialogue? In Portuguese,
the word for *Europe*, like with many countries, is used with a word for *the*
(**Europa** is feminine), so its literal meaning is: *through the Europe*.

How would you say: *along the avenue / through the park / along the
beaches*?

Practice 1

1 **Take part in the dialogue by following the prompts. You are
   discussing where you and your family spend your holidays.**

Teresa	Onde passa as férias em geral?
You	**(a)** *Say you often go to Italy in the spring* (**na primavera**).
Teresa	Por que gosta da Itália?
You	**(b)** *Say you like Italian culture.*
Teresa	E os filhos também vão?
You	**(c)** *Say that your son always comes with you, but that your daughter prefers to travel with her boyfriend.*
Teresa	Onde quer ir nas férias de inverno (*winter*)?
You	**(d)** *Say that you usually stay at home, but that you and your family want to get to know France in the autumn* (**no outono**).

2   09.03 **Now speak in the pauses and listen to confirm your
   answers.**

3 **Complete these sentences with the appropriate form of conhecer
   or saber.**
   a Sabes que horas são? Não _____.
   b A minha mãe _____ o teu irmão.
   c A Paula e a Susana não _____ falar italiano.
   d Vocês _____ o Brasil?
   e Eu _____ nadar muito bem.
   f Nós não _____ onde vamos passar as férias.

 Diálogo 2

Daniela and Lúcia are discussing where they would like to spend their holidays, and where they are going to spend them.

 1 09.04 **Listen to, and repeat the key expressions first.**

quinze dias	*fifteen days (a fortnight)*
diz	*he / she says*
no outono	*in the autumn*
para o ano	*next year*
gostaria de	*I would like (to)*
o dinheiro	*money*
provavelmente	*probably*
na terra	*in (one's) home town, region*

2 09.05 **Now listen to the dialogue, then answer the questions.**

  a Where is Daniela going on holiday this year? Can you work out which month?

Daniela	Lúcia, onde vais passar as férias este ano?
Lúcia	Pois, em março vou visitar a Inglaterra para passar tempo com a minha amiga inglesa. E tu, Daniela? Tens férias este ano?
Daniela	Tenho. Vou passar quinze dias na Espanha, em novembro. A minha mãe diz que é muito bonita no outono. O que vais fazer para o ano?
Lúcia	Bom, no ano que vem gostaria de viajar pela Índia. E tu?
Daniela	Também gostaria de fazer uma viagem exótica, mas não tenho muito dinheiro. Provavelmente no ano que vem vou passar as férias na terra, em Braga.

  b Where would Lúcia like to travel through next year? Why might Daniela not be able to fulfil her plans for an exotic journey?

3 Can you match up the Portuguese to the English?

  a março   **1** November

  b novembro   **2** an exotic journey

  c no ano que vem   **3** March

  d uma viagem exótica   **4** next year

Language discovery

1 OS MESES DO ANO *THE MONTHS OF THE YEAR*

 09.06 **Listen to the months and try to imitate the native pronunciation.**

janeiro	*January*
fevereiro	*February*
março	*March*
abril	*April*
maio	*May*
junho	*June*
julho	*July*
agosto	*August*
setembro	*September*
outubro	*October*
novembro	*November*
dezembro	*December*

Note that the months in Portuguese have small letters.

2 AS ESTAÇÕES *THE SEASONS*

09.07 **Now listen to the seasons and imitate the pronunciation.**

a primavera	*spring*
o verão	*summer*
o outono	*autumn*
o inverno	*winter*

 Which season is feminine?

3 NOW OR NEXT YEAR?

When you want to talk about things you do now, you use the simple parts of the verbs you have been learning – these are in the present time, i.e. what you are doing now, or what you usually do:

Sempre vou a uma aula de francês.   *I always go to a French class.*

If you want to talk about an action which is going to take place at some point in the future, be it near or far in time, you can simply use the appropriate part of the verb **ir** (*to go*), plus the action verb in exactly the same way we do in English.

| **Vamos visitar o Japão no ano vem.** | *We're going to visit Japan next year.* |
| **Vou à cidade amanhã.** | *I'm going to town tomorrow.* |

4 GOSTARIA (DE) … I WOULD LIKE (TO) …

You know already how to talk about things you like, using **gostar de**. If you want to discuss something you would like to do, then you must use the form used by Lúcia in the dialogue: **gostaria de viajar** (*I would like to travel*). The whole verb is:

eu	gostar**ia**	nós	gostar**íamos**
tu	gostar**ias**	eles / elas	gostar**iam**
ele / ela	gostar**ia**	os senhores / as senhoras	
o senhor / a senhora		vocês	
você			

| **O que gostaria de ver?** | *What would you like to see?* |
| **Gostaríamos de comprar um carro.** | *We would like to buy a car.* |

 How would you say: *He would like to paint the house; I'd like to travel by sea?*

 Practice 2

1 **Combine the words from each column to make six complete sentences. There is a variety of possible answers. Take care to match the correct verb form with the correct person form. You'll find some sample answers in the Key to the exercises.**

a	eu	vamos	trabalhar	pela Escócia	amanhã
b	tu	vão	jogar	no mar	no ano que vem
c	você	vou	tirar	no jardim	em julho
d	nós	vai	visitar	golfe	na sexta feira
e	os senhores	vão	nadar	férias	em abril
f	eles	vais	viajar	o meu amigo	no sábado

2 How would you say the following?

a I would like to visit Germany.

b Paulo would not like to work on Monday.

c Would you (pl) like to drink with us?

d My husband / wife would like to try Brazilian food.

e We would like to travel through America.

3 Língua viva – Study the train timetable: For which months is it valid?

COMBOIO DE FÉRIAS

PORTO-ALGARVE-PORTO

A partir de 30 de Junho até 10 de Setembro de 2014 realiza-se este serviço, com os horários e dias de circulação abaixo indicados:

20800/ /20801 ✕ Ⓡ 🚌 ① 1-2	20802/ /20803 ✕ Ⓡ 🚌 ② 1-2		ESTAÇÕES		20862/ /20863 ✕ Ⓡ 🚌 ③ 1-2	20864/ /20865 ✕ Ⓡ 🚌 ④ 1-2
6 30	20 45	P	Porto (Campanhã)	C	0 00	8 18
6 36	20 52		Vila Nova de Gaia		23 54	8 12
6 48	21 05		Espinho		23 41	7 58
7 15	21 33		Aveiro		23 12	7 27
7 47	22 10	C	Coimbra-B	P	22 38	6 53
7 48	22 12	P		C	22 36	6 52
8 52	23 16	C	Entroncamento	P	21 29	5 41
9 04	23 30	P		C	21 15	5 24
14 50	5 45	C	* Tunes *	P	15 18	22 47
14 54	5 53	P		C	15 08	22 41
15 03	6 03		Albufeira		15 02	22 35
15 18	6 20		Loulé		14 45	22 18
15 32	6 35	C	Faro	P	14 29	22 01
15 47	7 05	P		C	14 10	21 29
15 57	7 14		Olhão		14 01	21 20
16 20	7 43		Tavira		13 37	20 57
16 47	8 17		V. Real de S. António		13 10	20 26
16 50	8 20	C ▼	V. R. de S. Ant.-Guad.	P	13 05	20 20

* Ligações de e para o Ramal de Lagos. Consulte os Cartazes Horários n.ᵒˢ ⑫.

Go further

If you are confident in your use of Portuguese numbers so far, then you're ready to go a bit further. You finished at 100 (**cem**, **cento**) last time.

 09.08 **Listen to the next group.**

101 **cento e um, uma**	150 **cento e cinquenta**
102 **cento e dois, duas**	160 **cento e sessenta**
105 **cento e cinco**	170 **cento e setenta**
110 **cento e dez**	180 **cento e oitenta**
120 **cento e vinte**	190 **cento e noventa**
130 **cento e trinta**	199 **cento e noventa e nove**
140 **cento e quarenta**	

The pattern for the formation of these numbers is just the same as for the last group you learnt:

cento e trinta e seis   100 + 30 + 6 = 136

Don't forget, wherever one or two appear, you must decide on the masculine or feminine form. Portuguese currency is masculine (**o euro**), so you might pay **dois euros** for a beer, but if you wanted to buy 122 beers, then you would have to ask for **cento e vinte e duas cervejas**!

 Practice 3

1   09.09 **Practise some numbers and see how many countries you can remember from earlier units. Listen to some fun Eurovision results. After each result, say what you think the result is in English. You will hear the correct answer on the audio.**

2   **Say whether these sums are (C) correct or (I) incorrect.**
   a Cento e cinco + trinta e um = cento e trinta e seis
   b Cento e noventa – vinte = cento e quarenta
   c Setenta e dois + quinze = cento e vinte e dois
   d Cento e sessenta – cinquenta = cento e dez
   e Cento e oitenta e três – oitenta e três = cem

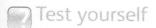
Test yourself

1 See if you can now do the following:

a Ask your friends where they're going on holidays this year.

b Say that you want to get to know Greece.

c Say that your family always spends its holidays in Portugal.

d Ask someone if they know how to swim.

e Say where you are going to spend your holiday next year.

f Ask someone if they would like to come too.

2 Complete the months and seasons:

a m_ _ç_

b _ _un_ _

c _ _ e_e_ _b_o

d _e_em_r_

e a_r_l

f _n_er_o

g o_t_n_

h _e_ _o

Transportes
Transport

In this unit you will learn how to:

▶ *discuss travelling and travel arrangements.*
▶ *talk about means of transport.*
▶ *use numbers from 200 upwards.*
▶ *give some orders.*
▶ *say 'more than' and 'less than'.*

CEFR: (A1) *Can handle numbers;* **(A2)** *can exchange limited information on familiar and routine operational matters.*

From tiny to huge

The Portuguese have a tendency to make words appear smaller, more affectionate, or friendly. This is done by modifying the endings, usually adding **-inho**, or **-zinho**, among others. A friendly **obrigadinha**, for example, comes from the more usual **obrigada**. You will hear many people use this form of thanks. Other common words of this type you may come across include: **coitadinho(a)**, from **coitado** (*poor thing*), and **pãozinho** (*bread roll*), from **pão**.

Conversely, some words are made larger by the addition of **-ão**; so if you wanted **uma garrafa de vinho** (*a bottle of wine*) but you asked for a **garrafão**, you'd probably get a five-litre flagon!

If **livro** is a *book*, can you figure out what *a small book* is?
If a **casinha** is *a small house*, what is the original word for *house*?
If a game is *a jogo*, what do you think is a really big football match in Brazil?

Diálogo 1

Olívia and Luísa are discussing how they travel to work.

1 10.01 **Listen to the new key expressions first.**

hoje	*today*
uma boleia	*a lift*
acho (que)	*I think (that)*
passar	*to pass (by)*
a empresa	*company, workplace*
obrigadinha (f)	*thanks very much*
o dentista	*the dentist*
vou de autocarro	*I'm going by bus*
vou a pé	*I'm going on foot*

2 10.02 **Now listen to the dialogue, first without looking at the text, and then by reading it a couple of times. Then answer the questions.**

a Does Luísa accept Olívia's offer of a lift?

Olívia	Bom dia, Luísa. Vais trabalhar hoje?
Luísa	Vou, sim.
Olívia	Queres uma boleia? Acho que vou passar à tua empresa.
Luísa	Obrigadinha, mas não. Hoje vou primeiro ao dentista. Vou de autocarro. Depois vou a pé para o trabalho.
Olívia	Muito bem. Então, até logo.

b Is Luísa going straight to work?
c How is she getting to work?

Diálogo 2

Senhor Pinto answers some questions about his commute to work.

1 10.03 **You will hear the key expressions first.**

como vai para o trabalho?	*how do you get to work?*
vou de comboio	*I go by train*
fora da cidade	*outside the city*
longe	*far away*
vou e volto	*I go and return*
queria comprar	*I would like to buy*
rápido	*fast*

barato	cheap
mais de	more than
quinhentos quilómetros	500 kilometres
uma reunião	a meeting

2 10.04 **Now listen to the conversation, then answer the questions.**

  a How do you say: *every day*?

Entrevistador	Senhor Pinto, como vai para o trabalho?
Sr Pinto	Bem, geralmente vou de comboio. O meu trabalho fica fora da cidade, um pouco longe. Vou e volto todos os dias.
Entrevistador	O senhor não tem carro?
Sr Pinto	Não tenho. Queria comprar, mas não tenho dinheiro, e o comboio é rápido e barato. Viajo mais de quinhentos quilómetros por semana.
Entrevistador	E vai sempre de comboio?
Sr Pinto	Às vezes vou de camioneta, e quando tenho uma reunião no Porto, vou de avião.

---

  b What does Sr Pinto say about the train?

  c What other means of transport does he use?

What words does Sr Pinto use to mean *by train*? Find the other examples of *I go by* in the dialogue.

Language discovery

1 DE CARRO, A PÉ *BY CAR, ON FOOT*

Means of transport is, in the main, conveyed by **de**, plus the name of the vehicle. Match the Portuguese and English expressions for transport:

a	de carro	**1**	by bike
b	de barco	**2**	by plane, air
c	de comboio	**3**	by underground (metro)
d	de bicicleta	**4**	by car
e	de autocarro	**5**	by boat
f	de moto(cicleta)	**6**	by train
g	de camioneta	**7**	by bus
h	de avião	**8**	by motorbike
i	de metro (metropolitano)	**9**	by coach

Queria is the polite form of the verb **querer** (*to wish, want*). You learnt this verb in the last unit. **Queria** is what you would use to ask for anything in a shop, ticket office, café, and so on. However, you also hear many Portuguese people use the verb in the present tense, especially when offering food or drinks, where in English you would probably use the polite form.

Queria um café, se faz favor.	*I'd like a coffee please.*
Quer comer alguma coisa?	*Do you want to eat anything? (Would you like anything to eat?)*
Não quero, não, obrigado.	*No thanks.*

3 MAIS DE, MENOS DE *MORE THAN, LESS THAN*

In Unit 4, you used **mais** (*more*) and **menos** (*less*) when talking about people being taller, shorter, or older than each other. When discussing numbers – be it prices, distances, time – more, or less than, is expressed by **mais de** and **menos de**.

Mais de cinquenta libras.	*More than £50.00*
Menos de dez minutos.	*Less than ten minutes.*

4 OS NÚMEROS 200 + *NUMBERS 200+*

If you are going to discuss distances you will need to be confident with numbers into the thousands. Who knows, if you played the **totoloto**, you could end up winning thousands of euros – and who's going to count your winnings if you can't? So, to help you on your way, here is the final group of numbers, from 200.

Listen and imitate the native pronunciation.

200	**duzentos**	800	**oitocentos**
300	**trezentos**	900	**novecentos**
400	**quatrocentos**	1,000	**mil**
500	**quinhentos**	2,000	**dois mil**
600	**seiscentos**	10,000	**dez mil**
700	**setecentos**	100,000	**cem mil**
	1,000,000	**um milhão**	

You can help yourself to learn numbers by looking for pattern-groups.

5 **cinco**	15 **quinze**	50 **cinquenta**	500 **quinhentos**
8 **oito**	18 **dezoito**	80 **oitenta**	800 **oitocentos**

The numbers in the hundreds (200, 300, 400, and so on) also have a feminine form, to be used when talking about large numbers of feminine items. If you wanted to say *400 miles*, you'd have to use **quatrocentas** with **milhas**.

The digits which make up the hundreds, tens, and units, are, in the main, divided in the same way as the last group you learnt – with the word **e** between each one. Hence, 953 would be: **novecentos e cinquenta e três**.

After thousands, there is usually no **e**. It only appears if the thousand is followed either by a numeral from 1 to 100, or by a numeral from 200 to 900 if the last two numbers are zeros.

1996 = **mil novecentos e noventa e seis**

2003 = **dois mil e três**

3600 = **três mil e seiscentos**

 Practice 1

1 **Complete the email using the words from the box.**

> volto   rápido   vou   férias   geral   dias   fins   gosto
> avião   de   barato   fora   bicicleta   barco

Em _____ vou para o trabalho _____ autocarro. Vou e _____ todos os _____ . O autocarro é _____ e bastante (*quite*) _____. Nos _____ de semana viajo _____ da cidade. _____ de comboio. Aos domingos _____ de passear de _____. Quando vou de _____, viajo de _____ ou de _____.

2 **10.06** **Listen to the list of numbers and see if you can repeat each one. Then write down what you think each number is.**

3 **Língua viva** – Which of the telephone numbers would you ring for information about buses?

> **AUTOCARROS.** Rua da República, 135. Tel. 23747/ 29624.
>
> **COMBOIOS.** Tel. 22125.
>
> **TÁXI-AÉREO.** Aeródromo de Évora. Tel. 28335.

4 **Read this advertisement from the classified section of a newspaper, and try answering the questions following it.**

> ## Vende-se bicicleta
>
> Está farto de viajar no carro dos seus amigos? Tenho uma bicicleta bonita que você vai querer comprar. Com uma bicicleta, pode-se chegar mais rápido ao trabalho, e melhorar a saúde. Só custa vinte euros. É barata! É bonita! Compre já!

  a What's for sale?
  b How much is it?
  c Name a benefit of having the item.

vende-se	*for sale*
está farto de ...?	*are you sick of ...?*
comprar	*to buy*
pode-se	*one can, you can*
melhorar	*to improve*
saúde	*health*
só custa	*it only costs*
compre já!	*buy now!*

Go further

1 MORE USES FOR REFLEXIVE VERBS

In Unit 7 you learnt some verbs, known as reflexives, which include the word *self* (**levanto-me**, **chamo-me**, and so on). You will find that reflexive verbs are used in other situations

Firstly, when something is for sale, rent, on offer, etc., the signs you see will say **vende-se** (*for sale*), **aluga-se** (*for rent*) or **oferece-se** (*on offer*). In the bike advertisement the actual vendor is not mentioned, so a bike for sale becomes a bike that 'sells itself' You will also come across shop or hotel sign which stress an action, but not the person performing it: **aqui fala-se inglês** (*English spoken here*).

Secondly, **pode-se** means *one can*, in the sense of *it is possible*, again this is a non-personalized form of the verb:

Pode-se fumar?   *Can one smoke?*

 How would you say: *Can one rent bicycles here?*

2 DE CARRO, NO CARRO DE RUI *BY CAR, IN RUI'S CAR*

Remember that means of transport are expressed by the word **de**. However, if you want to specify either someone's vehicle, or a timetabled train, bus, plane and so on, you will use **em** or **no**, **na** (*in / on the*).

no carro dos seus amigos	*in your friends' car*
no comboio das dez e meia	*on the 10.30 train*
no avião de TAP	*on the TAP plane*

3 COMPRE! *BUY!*

Ordering people to do things (however politely) can be rather complex in Portuguese, so for the moment just have a brief look at the polite (you) form. With regular verbs look at what happens. Here are three examples:

Infinitive		Present tense		Polite command	
comprar	*to buy*	**compra**	*you buy*	**compre!**	*buy!*
comer	*to eat*	**come**	*you eat*	**coma!**	*eat!*
partir	*to leave*	**parte**	*you leave*	**parta!**	*leave!*

 What is the pattern in which the verbs change?

To order more than one person, simply add an **-m** to the above forms (**comprem, comam, partam**).

Irregular verbs are awkward. Here are a few examples:

Infinitive		Singular	Plural	
fazer	to make / do	faça	façam	make / do
ser	to be	seja	sejam	be
estar	to be	esteja	estejam	be
ter	to have	tenha	tenham	have
ir	to go	vá	vão	go
vir	to come	venha	venham	come

You will pick up on other examples as you go along. In English these commands are usually followed by an extra word – more to give weight and rhythm to the command than for meaning. For example: *Have it! Go away! Come here!* Portuguese does the same: **Tome lá! Vá embora! Venha cá!**

 Practice 2

1 How would you say the following?

a I go to work in my friend's car.
b Paulo goes to the hospital by bus.
c Ana is travelling on the 2.30 p.m. train.
d Mr and Mrs da Costa are going on holiday by boat.
e We are going to the cinema on the 7.15 p.m. bus.
f Are you (**tu**) travelling by plane?

2 Supply the correct command forms to complete these sentences.

a (comprar – singular)   _____ o carro!
b (comer – plural)   _____ as sardinhas!
c (partir – plural)   _____ hoje!
d (viajar – singular)   _____ de comboio!
e (falar – plural)   _____ menos rápido!
f (beber – singular)   _____ o café!

Listen to six people describing how they tend to travel, and number the transports 1–6, according to the order in which they are mentioned.

bicycle _____   car _____   on foot _____
horse _____   coach _____   bus _____

Reading and writing

1 Read this blog about public transport.

> **Como vai para o trabalho? Debate internacional**
>
> Olá!
>
> Em Lisboa há vários transportes públicos que utilisamos para chegar ao trabalho. O metropolitano é rápido e eficiente. Os bilhetes são baratos. O sistema de autocarros também é muito bom aqui. Pode-se viajar de carro mas sempre há muito trânsito no centro de Lisboa. Eu viajo no carro da minha amiga. O meu amigo Jorge mora em Sintra e geralmente viaja de comboio – ele gosta de relaxar durante a viagem. A minha irmã mora perto do trabalho e vai a pé.
>
> E vocês? Como vão para o trabalho? Qual transporte preferem?
>
> Ana da Silva, Lisboa

2 Now add to the debate by providing the Portuguese for the words in brackets:

> Olá Ana!
>
> Em Londres também há _____ (*many*) transportes _____ (*public*). _____ (*I like*) de viajar de _____ (*underground*), mas os bilhetes são muito _____ (*expensive*). Prefiro apanhar _____ (*the bus*), mas quando tenho _____ (*a meeting*), _____ (*I go*) _____ (*by taxi*). É mais _____ (*fast*). Adoro ir _____ (*on foot*), mas _____ (*I don't live*) no centro da cidade; a minha casa é _____ (*far away*) do trabalho. _____ (*sometimes*) vou de _____ (*train*).
>
> Jackie West, Londres

1 Now see if you can do the following:
   a Ask someone if they want a lift.
   b Say that you generally travel by bus.
   c Say that you'd like a beer, please.
   d Say that the train is quite cheap.
   e Say that John travels on the 9 o'clock bus.
   f Tell your friends to 'eat the cake!'

2 Translate:
   a Venha cá!
   b alugam-se bicicletas
   c a saúde
   d é mais rápido
   e mais de duzentas libras
   f de camioneta
   g fora da cidade
   h um garrafão de água

3 Complete the sequences by supplying the missing number in Portuguese:

   a 200   300   400   _____
   b 900   850   800   _____
   c 5,000   6,000   7,000   _____
   d 610   620   630   _____
   e 390   380   370   _____

SELF CHECK

I CAN...
. . . discuss travelling and travel arrangements
. . . talk about means of transport
. . . use numbers from 200 upwards
. . . give some orders!
. . . say 'more than' and 'less than'

Viajar
Travelling

In this unit you will learn how to:

▶ *talk about using public transport.*
▶ *buy tickets.*
▶ *request information at the tourist office.*
▶ *ask for and understand directions.*

CEFR: (A2) *Can get simple information about travel, use public transport: buses, trains and taxis, ask and give directions, and buy tickets; **(A2)** can ask for and give directions referring to a map or plan.*

Using public transport

In Portugal **o transporte público** (*public transport*) is efficient and provides a good way to see more of the country and its people. Once you have learnt a few basic phrases for travelling, you will have a lot more confidence to get about.

Viajar de comboio (*to travel by train*) in Portugal is extremely cheap and trains usually run on time. Fares vary depending on when you travel: most stations have **folhetos de informação** (*information leaflets*) with **horários** (*timetables*) and **preços** (*prices*).

You can also travel by **camioneta** (*coach*). The long-distance coaches are very comfortable. You can usually only buy **um bilhete simples / de ida** (*single / one-way ticket*) and you have to buy **um bilhete de volta** (*return ticket*) at the **central rodoviária / central de camionagem** (*coach station*) on your return.

Now that you know the words for *tickets*, what do you think the expression **de ida e volta** means?

Diálogos 1

You will hear short exchanges taking place at various departure points for different means of transport.

1 11.01 **Familiarize yourself with the key vocabulary before you listen to the audio. Then, try to imitate the native pronunciation.**

NO AEROPORTO *AT THE AIRPORT*

a cidade	*town / city*
centro	*centre*
o senhor sai	*you leave / go out*
a paragem	*(bus) stop*
ali / lá	*there*
tomar	*to take*
a praça de táxis	*taxi rank*
lá fora	*out there*

11.02 **Preview the vocabulary then listen to five mini dialogues about various means of transport.**

Senhor	Faz favor, há autocarros para o centro da cidade?
Informações	Sim, há. O senhor sai do aeroporto e a paragem é ali em frente.
	Também pode tomar um táxi. A praça de táxis é lá fora.

NO PORTO *AT THE PORT*

porto	*port*
parte	*departs*
chega	*arrives*

Senhora	Desculpe, a que horas parte o barco para a Madeira?
Senhor	Às dez e quinze.
Senhora	E a que horas chega?
Senhor	Às quatro menos vinte da manhã.

a estação de comboios	*train station*
a estação de caminho de ferro (C.F.)	*railway station*
à esquerda	*on / to the left*

| **Senhora** | Faz favor, há uma estação de comboios aqui? |
| **Senhor** | Sim, a estação de caminho de ferro é ali, à esquerda. |

NA RUA (2)

à direita	*on / to the right*
apanhar	*to catch (bus, train, etc.)*
o terminal	*bus terminus*

| **Senhor** | Onde é a paragem de autocarros para Lagos? |
| **Senhora** | É ali, à direita. Também pode apanhar um autocarro do terminal, que é ali atrás da praça. |

NUM TÁXI *IN A TAXI*

para	*to / for*
o hotel	*hotel*
quanto é?	*how much is it?*
são ... euros	*it's / they are ... euros*

Turista	Para o hotel Vistamar, se faz favor.
Taxista	Muito bem.
Turista	Quanto é?
Taxista	São sete euros.

2 Now answer these questions:

  a How many means of transport are mentioned in the conversations?

  b What two expressions are used for train station?

Practice 1

1 How would you say the following?
   a Are there buses to Lisbon (**Lisboa**)?
   b The bus stop is over there on the left.
   c The taxi rank is there on the right.
   d What time does the train for Faro leave?
   e At 6.15 in the evening.
   f What time does the boat arrive?
   g Is there an airport here?
   h The bus terminus is over there, in front.
   i To the port, please.

Diálogo 2

Ana quer viajar de comboio. *Ana wants to travel by train.*

1 First listen to the new vocabulary.

um bilhete	*a ticket*
de ida / ida e volta	*single / return*
um rápido (-direto)	*an express (direct)*
muito bem	*very well*
qual?	*which?*
a linha	*platform*
de nada	*don't mention it*

2 Now listen to the conversation then answer the questions.
   a Where does Ana wish to travel?

Ana	Bom dia. Queria um bilhete para o Porto, se faz favor.
Senhor	Quer de ida ou de ida e volta?
Ana	Ida e volta.
Senhor	Primeira ou segunda classe?
Ana	Segunda faz favor. É um rápido?
Senhor	Há um rápido-direto às duas horas.
Ana	Qual é a linha?
Senhor	É a linha número quatro.
Ana	Obrigada.
Senhor	De nada, bom dia.

   b Does she buy a single or a return ticket?
   c Which expression means second class?

NA ESTAÇÃO DE CAMINHO DE FERRO *AT THE RAILWAY STATION*

1 Take part in this conversation by following the prompts.

You	*(a) Say good afternoon, I'd like two tickets to Loulé, please.*
Senhor	Quer de ida ou de ida e volta?
You	*(b) Return, please.*
Senhor	Primeira ou segunda classe?
You	*(c) First. Which platform is it to Loulé?*
Senhor	É a linha número um.
You	*(d) What time does the train leave?*
Senhor	Às oito menos dez.
You	*(e) And what time does it arrive?*
Senhor	Às nove e vinte e cinco.
You	*(f) Thank you.*
Senhor	De nada. Boa tarde.

2 Now speak in the pauses, then listen to confirm your answers.

3 Língua viva – Look at the two announcements then answer the questions.

   a Is the ticket on the right a single or return?

   b Is the ticket on the left 1st or 2nd class?

Caminhos de Ferro Portugueses		
TUNES **ALCANTARILHA**		
Preço € 5,85	2a classe	Inteiro Adulto

EVA Turismo

BILHETE SIMPLES
No: 18005 J

Tarifa: Euros – 7,50

De: Braga
Para: Coimbra

Conserve este bilhete

IVA INCLUÍDO

Diálogo 3

1 *11.06* **First, listen to the key expressions:**

tem ...?	*do you have ...?*
hotéis (um hotel)	*hotels (a hotel)*
pensões (uma pensão)	*guest houses (a guest house)*
nos arredores	*on the outskirts*
a região	*region*
as informações	*information*
as atrações	*attractions*

2 *11.07* **Now listen to the dialogue, then answer the questions.**

a Does the tourist already have a place to stay? How can you tell?

Turista	Tem uma lista de hotéis da cidade?
Senhora	Aqui tem uma lista de hotéis, pensões e albergues. Também há um parque de campismo nos arredores da cidade.
Turista	E tem uma planta da cidade?
Senhora	Temos esta, e um mapa da região.
Turista	E tem informações sobre a cidade, as lojas, as atrações...?
Senhora	Aqui tem.

uma lista	*a list*
os albergues	*hostels*
um parque de campismo	*a campsite*
uma planta	*a town plan*
um mapa	*a map*
as lojas	*shops*

b What types of accommodation are available in town?
c Where is there a campsite?
d Are town plans available from the tourist office?
e What do you think is the meaning of **Aqui tem**?

 Diálogos 4

Look at the town centre map as you listen to the following dialogues. Then listen again and answer the questions. You will hear the new vocabulary before each dialogue.

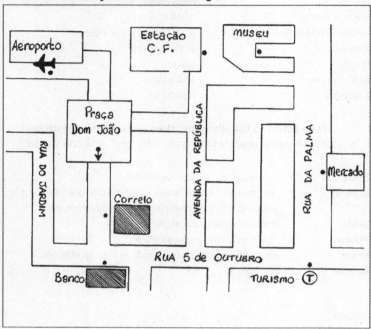

À PORTA DO TURISMO *OUTSIDE THE TOURIST OFFICE*

(onde) fica?	*(where) is (...) situated?*
vira, vire	*turn*
toma	*take*
segue, siga em frente	*carry straight on*
a rua	*road*

Senhor	Faz favor, onde fica a estação de caminho de ferro?
Transeunte	O senhor vira aqui à esquerda, toma a segunda rua à direita, segue sempre em frente, e a estação fica à esquerda.

a Is the station on the left or on the right?

112

perto (daqui)	*near (here)*
até (a)	*until / up to*
o correio	*post office*
à esquina	*on the corner*
sabe, sabes	*you know*

Senhora	Desculpe, sabe onde fica o banco?
Senhor	Sim. O banco é muito perto daqui. Siga sempre em frente até ao correio, depois vire à esquerda, e o banco é ali à esquina.

b What building is the lady looking for?

NO MERCADO *AT THE MARKET*

lá fora *(there)*	*outside*
o museu	*museum*
fácil	*easy*
vai	*go*
terceira (f)	*third*
mesmo ali	*right there*

Isabel	Nuno, tu sabes onde fica o museu?
Nuno	Sim. É muito fácil. Vai lá fora, vira à direita, e segue sempre em frente. Toma a terceira à esquerda e o museu fica mesmo ali em frente.

c What is the way to the museum?

Language discovery

1 GIVING DIRECTIONS

The main verbs used in directing people are: **tomar** (*to take*), **virar** (*to turn*), **seguir** (*to follow*) and **ir** (*to go*).

Toma a segunda rua.	*You take the second road.*
Vire aqui à esquerda.	*Turn left there.*

Depending on how well you know the person, the verb endings may well differ.

	very polite	polite (você, etc.) – use verb on its own	familiar (tu) – use verb on its own
use o senhor a senhora, or você + verb	toma vira segue vai	tome vire siga vá	toma vira segue vai

The last two columns are known as commands. As you will mainly be listening to directions, the main thing is to focus on understanding the direction, and not worry too much about the verb ending at this stage.

Practice 3

1 Now follow these directions and see if you can discover where you have been sent.

   a Start at the **museu**: Siga em frente e vire à direita. Depois vá em frente e o _____ fica à esquerda.

   b Start at the **banco**: Vá lá fora e vire à direita. Tome a primeira à esquerda e siga sempre em frente, até à _____ que fica à esquerda.

   c Start at the **estação**: Vire à direita e vá sempre em frente. Tome a segunda à esquerda. Depois siga sempre em frente e o _____ fica à direita.

2 11.09 **Listen to the instructions you hear and complete the directions.**

Faz favor, onde fica _____ _____?
Bem, a senhora _____ aqui _____ _____, e _____ a _____
rua _____ _____ _____ _____ _____ até _____
_____, e _____ _____ fica _____ _____. Obrigada.

3 Complete these expressions with words connected with travel.

   a um bilhete de ida e _____

   b a estação de _____ de ferro

   c a paragem de _____

   d _____ o Hotel Campoverde, se faz favor.

   e primeira ou segunda _____

   f a que _____ parte o comboio?

1   What do the following phrases mean?

  a à esquerda
  b à direita
  c Ida e volta
  d Qual é a linha?
  e Tem?
  f nos arredores
  g Onde fica?
  h siga em frente
  i perto
  j lá fora

2   In each list, there is a word that does not belong. Can you find it?

a comboio	estação de CF	terminal	linha
b à esquerda	a lista	à direita	em frente
c hotel	folheto	mapa	planta
d ida	ida e volta	preço	bilhete
e albergue	paragem	pensão	hotel

3   Follow the English prompts to take part in a conversation at the Tourist Office. Speak in the pauses and listen to check your answers:

You	(a) *Good morning. Do you have a map of the region?*
Senhor	Bom dia. Sim, temos. Aqui tem.
You	(b) *Thanks. Do you also have a list of guest houses please?*
Senhor	Tome. Também tem uma planta da cidade.
You	(c) *Where is the train station?*
Senhor	Vire à esquerda e siga sempre em frente.
You	(d) *Thanks very much.*

SELF CHECK

	I CAN...
○	. . . talk about using public transport
○	. . . buy tickets
○	. . . request information at the tourist office
○	. . . ask for and understand directions

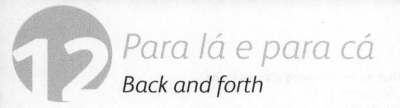

Para lá e para cá
Back and forth

In this unit you will learn how to:

▶ *get money, buy stamps and make phone calls.*
▶ *recognize public signs and road information.*
▶ *clarify where you are going.*
▶ *report accidents and theft.*

CEFR: (A2) *Can ask about things and make simple transactions in shops, post offices or banks;* **(A2)** *can understand enough to manage simple, routine exchanges without undue effort.*

Services and facilities

Most Portuguese tourist areas have modern banks, with services such as the **multibanco** (*ATM*). Although you can opt for the instructions in English, the following may be useful: you have to **introduzir** (*insert*) your **cartão bancário** (*bank card*), you may need to **anular** (*cancel*) or **corrigir** (*correct*) what you have done. Inside the bank you may find a **o câmbio** (*exchange*) sign on the counter. Portugal uses **o euro** (*the euro*), which is divided into 100 **cêntimos** (*cents*).

For your **telemóvel** (*mobile phone*), you may need to buy a **carregador** (*charger*). If you have to **fazer uma chamada** (*make a call*) from a public phone, find **uma cabine telefónica** (*a telephone box*) – they are operated by phone cards available at post offices, newsagents and street kiosks.

When out and about in your car, you may come across the **GNR – Guarda Nacional Republicana** (*National Guard*) or the **Brigada do Trânsito** (*Traffic Police*). If you are the victim of car theft, you will need to report it at the local **Esquadra da Polícia** (*police station*).

What do you think the verb **cambiar** means?
If a **cartão bancário** is a *bank card*, what do you think these are: **cartão telefónico / cartão de memória?**

Diálogo 1

NO BANCO *IN THE BANK*

The cash machine is out of service, so a customer enters the bank to make a cash withdrawal.

1 12.01 **First listen to the new key expressions and repeat them after the speaker:**

levantar	*to take out, withdraw money*
o dinheiro	*money*
o cartão	*card*
quanto ... ?	*how much ... ?*
faça favor de ...	*please ...*
preencher	*to fill in, complete*
este formulário	*this form*
já está	*there we are, there it is (lit. already it is)*
ora bem	*right then*

2 12.02 **Now listen to the conversation. How much money does the lady want to withdraw?**

Senhora	Posso levantar dinheiro com o meu cartão aqui? A máquina está avariada.
Clerk	Com certeza. Quanto queria?
Senhora	100 (cem) euros, se faz favor.
Clerk	Um momento, sim? Tem passaporte?
Senhora	Aqui está.
Clerk	Faça favor de preencher este formulário: nome, morada aqui em Portugal, número do cartão.
Senhora	Já está.
Clerk	Ora bem. *(counting the money)* 20 (vinte), 40 (quarenta), 60 (sessenta), 80 (oitenta), 100 (cem) euros.
Senhora	Obrigada.
Clerk	De nada. Bom dia.

3 Can you complete the English meanings of these words from the conversation?

a máquina	_____
avariada (f)	broken down
com certeza	of course, certainly
um momento	one _____
o passaporte	_____

 Diálogo 2

AO CORREIO *AT THE POST OFFICE*

1 12.03 **Listen to the key expressions first.**

um selo	*a stamp*
para cartas / postais	*for letters / postcards*
ao todo	*in total, all*

2 12.04 **Now listen to the conversation at the post office. How many letters does the lady wish to send?**

Sandra	Olá, queria oito selos para Inglaterra, e dois para Alemanha, se faz favor.
Senhora	São para cartas, ou postais?
Sandra	Três cartas e sete postais.
Senhora	Bom, são seis euros ao todo.

 Practice 1

1 Match up the questions (a–e) with the replies (1–5).

a	Qual é a sua morada aqui em Portugal?	**1**	200 euros, se faz favor.
b	Para cartas, ou postais?	**2**	É o apartamento Sol, Praça São João, Loulé.
c	Quanto queria?	**3**	Com certeza.
d	Posso levantar dinheiro?	**4**	Para cinco cartas.
e	Tem passaporte?	**5**	Aqui está.

2 Can you guess what these public signs and notices mean in English?

a PARA CRIANÇAS	**e** PERIGO
b NÃO FUMAR	**f** SAÍDA DE EMERGÊNCIA
c PROIBIDO ESTACIONAR	**g** ENTRADA PROIBIDA
d ABERTO DAS 10.00 ÀS 12.00	**h** FECHADO

3 **Língua viva – Look at the sign and answer the questions about it.**

Proibido Estacionar
entre as 13.00 e as
15.00 horas.

Saída de Emergência
Lojas Primavera.

a   What can you not do here?

b   Why not?

c   Whose reserved space is it?

TOILETS!

Public conveniences are difficult to find in Portugal. It is common practice to use the toilet in a bar, café (where you may need to get the key first) or even a hotel. There are various names for toilets:

a casa de banho	*bathroom*	**a sanita**	*toilet bowl*
os sanitários	*public toilets*	**os lavabos**	*washroom and toilet*
a retrete	*separate toilet*		

4 **Find the missing words from each phrase below, and fit them onto the crossword grid.**

1 Posso fazer uma _____?
2 Tem _____?
3 Qual é a sua _____ em Portugal?
4 Sete _____ para Espanha, por favor.
5 10 _____ ao todo.
6 Posso _____ dinheiro?
7 Para _____ ou postais?
8 _____ telefónica

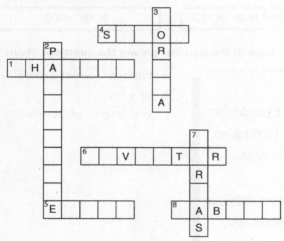

5 **Now take part in a dialogue at a post office by following the English prompts.**

You	**(a)** *Say: good afternoon, I would like five stamps for England please.*
PO clerk	Para cartas ou postais?
You	**(b)** *Say: for postcards.*
PO clerk	É tudo?
You	**(c)** *Say: no, I'd also like two stamps for the USA for postcards. That's all.*
PO clerk	Muito bem, então são 4 euros e 60 por favor
You	**(d)** *Say: thank you.*

6   12.05   **Now speak in the pauses, then listen to confirm your answers.**

NA ESTRADA *ON THE HIGHWAY*

Miguel pede informações sobre o caminho para a Nazaré. *Michael asks for directions to Nazaré.*

1 12.06 **Listen to the key expressions first.**

o caminho certo	*the right way*
era melhor	*it would be better*
a saída	*exit*
vai demorar muito?	*is it going to take a long time?*
a Nazaré fica a 80 quilómetros daqui	*Nazaré is 80 km away*
acho que não	*I don't think so*
mais ou menos	*more or less*
é um instantinho	*it's really quick*

2 12.07 **Now listen to the conversation. How far from Nazaré is Michael?**

Miguel	Desculpe, é este o caminho certo para a Nazaré?
Senhora	Ah, não é exatamente, não. Era melhor seguir por esta estrada até à rotunda, e ali tomar a segunda saída, e seguir por aquele caminho.
Miguel	Vai demorar muito?
Senhora	Acho que não. A Nazaré fica a oitenta quilómetros daqui, mais ou menos. Se seguir a estrada A1, vai logo ver os sinais para a Nazaré. É um instantinho.
Miguel	Muito obrigado e bom dia.

exatamente	*exactly*
a estrada	*road, highway*
a rotunda	*roundabout*
se seguir	*if you follow*
a estrada A1	*national highway A1*
vai logo ver	*you'll soon see*
os sinais	*road signs*

Can you work out how to say *It's going to take a minute*?
If **acho que não** means *I don't think so*, can you work out how to say *I think so*?

1 CONHECER, SABER *TO KNOW*

There are two verbs in Portuguese that mean to know (you met them previously in Unit 9). You'll no doubt remember that **conhecer** means *to know a person or place*, and **saber** means *to know a fact*. You will need these verbs when out and about, especially if you want to ask people for information:

Sabe que horas são?	*Do you know what time it is?*
Sabe o caminho certo para Lisboa?	*Do you know the right way to Lisbon?*
Conhece a cidade de Braga?	*Do you know (are you familiar with) the city of Braga?*
Não conheço por nome.	*I don't recognize by name.*

Here are the two verbs in the present tense.

	conhecer	saber
eu	**conheço**	**sei**
tu	**conheces**	**sabes**
ele, ela você o Sr / a Sra	**conhece**	**sabe**
nós	**conhecemos**	**sabemos**
eles, elas vocês os Srs / as Sras	**conhecem**	**sabem**

Practice 2

1 **Decide which of the two verbs, saber or conhecer should go in each sentence. The correct form is provided in brackets to help you.**

   a A Maria _____ o meu irmão. (sabe / conhece)

   b Nós não _____ as horas. (sabemos / conhecemos)

   c Tu queres _____ a França? (conhecer / saber)

   d Eles _____ o Presidente. (sabem / conhecem)

   e O João não _____ o meu nome. (conhece / sabe)

Diálogo 4

A ESTAÇÃO DE SERVIÇO *THE SERVICE STATION*

O Senhor Neto quer comprar gasolina. *Mr Neto wants to buy some petrol.*

1 12.08 **Listen to the key expressions and try to imitate the native speaker.**

a gasolina	*petrol*
sem chumbo	*unleaded petrol*
o gasóleo, o óleo	*diesel, oil*
quantos litros?	*how many litres?*
pode encher o depósito	*you can fill the tank*
pôr	*to put*
o ar	*air*
aceita / aceitamos	*(you) accept / we accept*
os cartões de crédito	*credit cards*

2   12.09   **Now listen to the dialogue, then answer the questions.**

Senhor Neto	Boa tarde. Quero gasolina, se faz favor.
Attendant	Claro. Quer sem chumbo ou gasóleo?
Senhor Neto	Sem chumbo.
Attendant	Quantos litros?
Senhor Neto	Pode encher o depósito. Preciso também de pôr ar nos pneus, e quero dois litros de óleo, por favor.
Attendant	Muito bem.
Senhor Neto	Aceita cartões de crédito?
Attendant	Aceitamos, sim.

a What kind of petrol does Sr Neto want?
b How much does he ask for?
c What else does he need?
d How does he pay?

3 Can you match up the Portuguese and English signs?

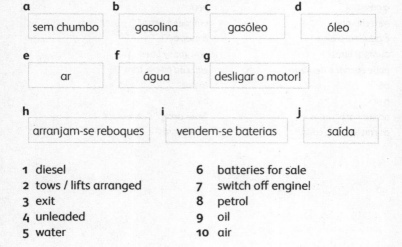

a	b	c	d
sem chumbo	gasolina	gasóleo	óleo

e	f	g
ar	água	desligar o motor!

h	i	j
arranjam-se reboques	vendem-se baterias	saída

1	diesel	**6**	batteries for sale
2	tows / lifts arranged	**7**	switch off engine!
3	exit	**8**	petrol
4	unleaded	**9**	oil
5	water	**10**	air

Diálogo 5

A senhora Johnson informa a Polícia sobre um roubo. *Mrs Johnson reports a theft to the police.*

1 12.10 **Listen to the key expressions first:**

que coisas?	*which things?*
uma mala que continha ...	*a bag which contained ...*
a carteira	*purse, wallet*
como aconteceu?	*how did it happen?*
corre um grande risco	*you run a big risk*
deixar	*to leave / leaving*
só demorei um pouco	*I was only a little while*

2 12.11 **Now listen to the conversation at the police station, then answer the questions.**

   a From where were the stolen items taken?

Senhora Johnson	Bom dia. Chamo-me Sylvia Johnson e sou inglesa. Estou aqui de férias. Quero comunicar o roubo dalgumas coisas no meu carro.
Polícia	Que coisas?
Senhora Johnson	A minha máquina fotográfica, o meu telemóvel, e uma mala que continha o meu passaporte e carteira com dinheiro.
Polícia	Como aconteceu?
Senhora Johnson	O vidro está partido.
Polícia	A senhora não sabe que corre um grande risco, deixar objetos dentro do carro?
Senhora Johnson	Eu sei, mas só demorei um pouco.
Polícia	Vai ter de preencher esta ficha em triplicado.

comunicar	*to report*
o roubo	*theft*
a máquina fotográfica	*camera*
partido	*broken*
os objetos	*objects*
a ficha	*form*
em triplicado	*in triplicate*

   b How did the thieves get into the car?
   c What was inside Mrs Johnson's bag?

Test yourself

1 What do the following phrases mean?
- **a** com certeza
- **b** faça favor de ...
- **c** para postais
- **d** ao todo
- **e** os lavabos
- **f** a rotunda
- **g** a estrada
- **h** os sinais
- **i** em triplicado

2 How would you say the following?
- **a** address
- **b** to fill in
- **c** I would like
- **d** a phone call
- **e** money

3 Choose the correct words to complete this dialogue about travelling to Tomar.
- **a** É este o caminho / sinal certo para Tomar?
- **b** Era melhor levantar / seguir por aquela estrada.
- **c** Vai demorar / preencher muito?
- **d** Acho que sim. Tomar fica a 250 km daqui. É muito longe / perto.
- **e** Se seguir a praça / estrada A25, vai ver os sinais.

4 **Look at the police notes of a reported crime and decide if the statements (a–e) are True or False.**

Nome:	Becker, H
Nacionalidade:	alemã
Crime:	roubo
Onde:	Restaurante Bom Comer
Quais objetos:	carteira com 80 Euros, telemóvel
Como aconteceu:	deixar ... objetos ... casa de banho ...

a The victim is German.
b The crime took place outside.
c A camera was taken.
d Money went missing.
e Items were taken from the bathroom.

SELF CHECK

I CAN...

○	. . . get money, buy stamps and make phone calls
○	. . . recognize public signs and road information
○	. . . clarify where I am going
○	. . . report accidents and theft

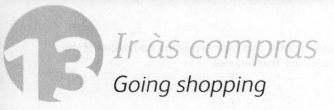

Ir às compras
Going shopping

In this unit you will learn how to:
▶ *buy produce at a market.*
▶ *deal with shops.*
▶ *recognize clothing terms.*

CEFR: (A1) *Can handle numbers related to quantities, costs, and time;* **(A2)** *can make simple purchases by stating what is wanted and asking the price*

 Shopping

Shopping in Portugal can be a great learning experience, and lots of fun, especially if you look for fresh produce at **o mercado** (*the market*), or if you try haggling for **uma pechincha** (*a bargain*) at **a feira** (*the weekly or monthly market*). Larger cities now have supermarket chains, as well as **centros comerciais** (*shopping centres*), or **hipermercados** (*hypermarkets*), and all towns have at least a few **minimercados** (*minimarts*). However, to practise the language, you need to venture into **as lojas** (*the shops*), where you will have direct contact with the Portuguese people. That may be to buy food in a small **mercearia** (*grocer's*), clothes in a **loja de roupas** (*clothes store*) or some lovely locally-made sandals in a **sapataria** (*shoe shop*).

So, **vamos às compras!** *Let's go shopping!*

 From the information above, can you work out the Portuguese for *a supermarket*?

Diálogo 1

AO MERCADO *AT THE MARKET*

1 13.01 **Listen to the key expressions first.**

as laranjas	*oranges*
o meio quilo	*1/2 kilo*
hoje	*today*
que mais?	*what else?*
quantas?	*how many?*
as pêras	*pears*
dê-me	*give me*
maduras (f / pl)	*ripe*
os quilos	*kilos*
é tudo	*that's all*
as cenouras	*carrots*

2 13.02 **Now listen to the conversation at the market stall, and read along. Then answer the questions.**

    a How many items does Mrs Silva buy?

Senhora Silva	Bom dia, minha senhora. Tem laranjas hoje?
Vendedora	Tenho, sim. Quantas quer?
Senhora Silva	Dê-me dois quilos se faz favor. E há cenouras?
Vendedora	Há, sim.
Senhora Silva	Bom, pois, eu quero meio quilo.
Vendedora	Que mais?
Senhora Silva	Também queria umas pêras. Estão boas hoje?
Vendedora	Estão boas, mas um pouco maduras.
Senhora Silva	Ah, maduras não quero. Está bem, então é tudo.

    b The **vendedora** asks Sra Silva how many oranges she wants (**quantas quer?**). What word would she have used to ask how many (kilos)?

    c Why doesn't Sra Silva want the pears?

 Vocabulary

If you are buying produce at the market, you may need some of the following vocabulary.

Legumes	Vegetables	Frutas	Fruit
as batatas	potatoes	os morangos	strawberries
o repolho	cabbage	as bananas	bananas
o pimentão	green pepper	a melancia	watermelon
as cebolas	onions	o ananás	pineapple
os cogumelos	mushrooms	as ameixas	plums
a alface	lettuce	as maçãs	apples
Peixe	*Fish*	**Carne**	*Meat*
o atum	tuna	o peru	turkey
o carapau	mackerel	o frango	chicken
o bacalhau	salted cod	o cabrito	kid
o espadarte	swordfish	o javali	wild boar
a pescada	hake	o leitão	suckling pig
as lulas	squid	o fígado	liver

 To which food categories do you think these belong? Can you guess what they are?

a couve-flor   a sardinha   o limão   a carne de porco   o melão
os mariscos   os tomates   o carne de vaca

When buying meat, you might need some names of different cuts:

a costeleta	chop
o escalope	scallop (thick sliced)
o entrecosto	entrecôte
a fatia	slice (thin)
uma asa	a wing
uma coxa	chicken drumstick / thigh

And don't forget your weights (in metric of course!)

13.03 **Listen to these weight measures, then try to imitate the speakers asking for various items at the market.**

um quilo de	*a kilo of*
meio quilo de	*half a kilo of*
250 gramas de	*250 g of*
100 gramas de	*100 g of*

How would you say: *a kilo of potatoes, 250 g of seafood, half a kilo of plums, 100 g of liver?*

Diálogo 2

NA MERCEARIA *IN THE GROCER'S SHOP*

1 **13.04** **Listen to the key expressions and try to imitate the native pronunciation.**

diga lá	*tell (me) then*
a meia dúzia	*half a dozen*
um pacote	*a packet*
uma garrafa	*a bottle*
ao fundo	*at the back*
mais alguma coisa?	*anything else?*

2 **13.05** **Now listen to the conversation in the grocer's shop. Then answer the questions.**

a How much milk does the customer ask for?

Freguesa *(customer)*	Boa tarde, senhor Maurício, como está?
Senhor Maurício	Bem, obrigado. E a senhora?
Freguesa	Estou bem. Olhe, preciso de comprar algumas coisas.
Senhor Maurício	Então, diga lá.
Freguesa	Quero meia dúzia de ovos, um litro de leite magro, um pacote de manteiga e uma garrafa de azeite *(she waits whilst being served)*.
	Pode cortar-me cinco fatias deste presunto aqui? E quanto é aquele queijo lá ao fundo?
Senhor Maurício	Aquele queijo da Serra custa sete euros e cinquenta o quilo.
Freguesa	Ah, então, dê-me trezentos gramas por favor.
Senhor Maurício	Mais alguma coisa?
Freguesa	É só. Obrigada. Quanto é?
Senhor Maurício	Ora bem, são cinco euros e cinquenta ao todo.

os ovos	*eggs*
o leite (magro)	*(skimmed) milk*
a manteiga	*butter*
o azeite	*olive oil*
o presunto	*smoked ham (boiled ham = fiambre)*
o queijo (da Serra)	*(Serra) cheese*
custa	*costs*

b What does the customer want five slices of?
c What's the total cost?

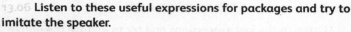 Vocabulary

13.06 Listen to these useful expressions for packages and try to imitate the speaker.

uma caixa de fósforos	*a box of matches*
um frasco de mel	*a jar of honey*
uma garrafa de vinho	*a bottle of wine*
um garrafão de água	*a demijohn of water*
uma lata de ervilhas	*a tin, can of peas*
uma barra de sabão	*a bar of soap*
um pacote de bolachas	*a packet of biscuits*
um tubo de pasta dentífrica	*a tube of toothpaste*
um rolo de papel higiénico	*a roll of toilet paper*
um pote de geleia	*a pot, jar of jam*

Practice 1

1 Alice has got her shopping list in a muddle, so her items and quantities are jumbled. Can you match the items correctly?

um quilo de	presunto
3 costeletas de	água
6 fatias de	cenouras
um pacote de	bolachas
2 latas de	pasta dentífrica
uma garrafa de	porco
um tubo de	sopa
uma dúzia de	ovos

2 Língua viva – Mandy wanted to buy some tuna. Did she get any? Check her till receipt to see if she bought some.

```
        SUPERMERCADO SILVA
      LARGO DE SANTA MARIA, 26
      7645 VILA NOVA MILFONTES
          CONT. N.801661528

   C    1      SCONTR     367
                          EUROS
   AGUA CRUZE 17%          0,37
   ATUM CALVO 17%          0,55
          2     X 0,40
   IOG. PEDAC. 17%         0,80
   PLANTA 250 17%          1,67
   **TOTAL**               3,39
   NUMERARIO               5,00
   TROCO                   1,61

   CAIXA 3    UNID     5
             OBRIGADO

        07-08-2014  17:05
```

Listening and reading

1 13.07 **Here is a passage all about buying clothes. You will hear some key expressions first. Listen and repeat each one, concentrating on the pronunciation.**

a casa de modas	*fashion house*
as roupas para ...	*clothes for ...*
os homens	*men*
as mulheres	*women*
como também	*as well as*
na moda	*in fashion*
além de	*as well as*
escolhe	*she chooses*
experimenta	*she tries (on)*

2 13.08 **Now listen carefully as you read along. What kind of footwear can you buy at this shop?**

Na Casa de Modas Silvana há roupas para homens (calças, camisas, gravatas, jaquetas) e para mulheres (vestidos, blusas, saias, conjuntos), como também os bonitos sapatos, sandálias e botas que estão na moda. Há roupas em vários estilos, cores e tamanhos. A senhora Ferreira quer comprar uma blusa. Há muitas cores – vermelho, amarelo, rosa, branco, preto e laranja, além de azul-claro e verde-escuro. A senhora Ferreira escolhe uma blusa em preto, depois experimenta um par de sapatos de salto alto, de cabedal.

as calças	*trousers*
os conjuntos	*suits (ladies)*
os estilos, o padrão	*styles, style*
os tamanhos	*sizes*
um par	*a pair*
de salto alto	*high heeled*
de cabedal	*in leather*

3 **Now that you've practised the vocabulary, can you answer these questions based on the Reading passage?**

   a Are there any children's clothes at the Casa Silvana?

   b What does Mrs Ferreira want to buy?

   c What colour does she choose?

   d What type of shoes does she try on?

4 **A department store wishes to put up bilingual signs to help its international customers. Decide which three items of clothing and footwear belong under each sign.**

a

> **Secção de mulheres** *Womenswear*
>
> 1 _____
>
> 2 _____
>
> 3 _____

b

> **Secção de homens** *Menswear*
>
> 1 _____
>
> 2 _____
>
> 3 _____

c | **Secção de calçado** *Footwear*

1 _____

2 _____

3 _____

1 sapatos	2 camisas	3 gravatas	4 jaquetas	5 vestidos
6 blusas	7 saias	8 sandálias	9 botas	

AS CORES *COLOURS*

 Sra Ferreira chooses **uma blusa em preto** *a blouse in black*; using what you learnt previously about adjectives, how would you say *a black blouse?*

vermelho	red
amarelo	yellow
(cor de) rosa	pink
branco	white
preto	black
(cor de) laranja	orange
azul-claro	light blue
verde-escuro	dark green

All colours can be used as adjectives, changing their endings where necessary; the general patterns are:

masculine	masc. plural	feminine	fem. plural
branco	brancos	branca	brancas
azul	azuis	azul	azuis
verde	verdes	verde	verdes

The expressions for *pink* and *orange* can be used with or without **cor de** (*colour of*), but don't need to change their endings.

 How would you say: *red shoes, a green tie, a pink skirt?*

 Practice 2

1 13.09 **Follow the prompts and take part in this dialogue at the grocer's shop. Listen to the audio to confirm your answers.**

Senhor Renato	Bom dia!
You	**(a)** *Say hello. I would like a litre of water and a loaf of sliced bread.*
Senhor Renato	Só temos este pão.
You	**(b)** *That's all right. I'll take one. Do you have smoked ham?*
Senhor Renato	Sim, temos este, que é bom.
You	**(c)** *Well, can you cut me six slices, please?*
Senhor Renato	Que mais?
You	**(d)** *I also want a tin of peas and a bar of soap.*
Senhor Renato	Mais?
You	**(e)** *That's all, thanks. How much is it?*

2 13.10 **Listen to various people doing their shopping. Complete the table below with the item they purchase, the quantity, and how much it costs. You will hear the answers on the recording.**

Person	Name of item	Quantity	Price
1			
2			
3			
4			
5			

136

1 Give the correct words for:

  a kilo
  b that's all
  c it costs
  d a bottle
  e in black
  f blouse
  g hake
  h a chop
  i soap
  j a pair

2 In each list there is a word that does not belong. Can you find it?

a repolho	tomates	alface	sardinhas
b atum	lulas	ananás	pescada
c morangos	cabrito	melancia	limão
d cogumelos	peru	javali	porco
e costeleta	entrecosto	lata	fatia
f fósforos	mel	papel higiénico	sabão

SELF CHECK

I CAN...

  ... buy produce at a market

  ... deal with shops

  ... recognize clothing terms

Comer fora
Eating out

In this unit you will learn how to:
▶ *order food in a café or restaurant.*
▶ *recognize typical Portuguese food and drink.*
▶ *interpret menus.*

CEFR: (A2) *Can order a meal;* **(A2)** *can find specific, predictable information in simple everyday material such as menus*

Eating and drinking out

There are plenty of places in Portugal where you can eat and drink. If you just want a snack, go to **um café** (*café*) or **um café-bar** (*coffee-bar*) or **uma pastelaria** (*a cake shop*). For main meals you could choose a **restaurante** (*restaurant*), a **casa de pasto** (*cheap diner*) or a **tasca** – a more basic bar – where you can buy a drink straight from the barrel, especially **cerveja** (*beer*).

Ask for **uma imperial** for a small draught Portuguese beer, or **um fino** in the north of Portugal, and **uma caneca** for a pint glass. **Vinho** (*wine*) is the thing to drink in Portugal, as it is inexpensive and, in the main, of excellent quality. There are some superb regions producing amazing **vinho tinto** (*red wine*), particularly in the Alentejo and the central Beiras. The city of **O Porto** (*Oporto*) is at the heart of the port wine industry with its historic links with English merchants. Northern Portugal produces the deliciously fruity young wine known as **vinho verde** (*green wine*).

Using information from the text, can you work out what these mean?
vinho branco   **vinho verde tinto**   **vinho rosé**   **vinho do Porto**

Diálogo 1

Paulo e os amigos entram na pastelaria Suíça. *Paulo and his two friends go into the Suíça cake shop.*

1 14.01 **Listen to the key expressions before you start.**

um galão	*a milky coffee*
um pastel de bacalhau	*a cod / potato fish cake*
uma bica	*a small black coffee*
uma sandes	*a sandwich*
os pastéis de nata	*custard cakes*
um sumo de laranja	*a fresh orange juice*
um quarto	*a 25 cl bottle*
com	*with*
sem	*without*
fresca (f)	*ice cold*

2 14.02 **Now listen to the conversation at the cake shop, then answer the questions.**

   a What drinks do the friends order?

Empregado	Boa tarde, que desejam?
Paulo	Pois, para mim, um galão e um pastel de bacalhau.
Nuno	Eu queria uma bica e uma sandes de queijo.
Empregado	E para a menina?
Maria	Tem pastéis de nata?
Empregado	Temos, sim.
Maria	Então dê-me dois, se faz favor.
Empregado	E para beber?
Maria	Um sumo de laranja.
Empregado	Mais alguma coisa?
Paulo	Pode ser também um quarto de água mineral.
Empregado	Com ou sem gás?
Paulo	Sem, e fresca. Obrigado.
Empregado	Muito bem.

   b How does the waiter address Paulo's friend Maria?
   c What expression is used in ordering to mean *it'll also be*?

In Portuguese, **café** means both the beverage and the place where you drink it. The Portuguese love their caffeine, which is reflected in the various expressions for the drink: ask for **um café** and you will get *a strong black espresso*. In southern Portugal you will also hear the term **uma bica**, and around the Porto area, you may come across **um cimbalino** (named after the Italian make of coffee machine). It is common to ask for a glass of water to accompany this strong shot! *A small, white coffee* is **um garoto**, and if you don't want that too milky, ask for **um pingado**. *A large white coffee* is either **uma meia de leite**, or simply **um café com leite**, and a very milky version served in a glass is a **galão**. Whichever way you take it, be sure to have a scrumptious **bolo** (*cake*) with it! Oh, and for those tea drinkers amongst you, you'll need to ask for **um chá com leite** (*white tea*), or **um chá com limão** (*tea with lemon*), or even indulge in **um chá-Lipton** (*iced tea*).

 Practice 1

1 **The waiter has brought a tray of snacks and drinks to the table but has forgotten who ordered what. Can you help by repeating each person's order once more? Simply state the items they wish to order:**

  a Paulo wants a black coffee, ham sandwich and custard cake.
  b Nuno wants a milky coffee, cheese sandwich, cod cake and custard cake.
  c Ana wants a fresh orange juice, ham sandwich and two cod cakes.
  d Maria wants a small slightly milky coffee, ham sandwich and two custard cakes.
  e Miguel wants a mineral water, one cod cake and one custard cake.

 14.03 **Now listen to confirm you said it correctly.**

Diálogo 2

Nuno e Miguel estão com pressa e querem comer alguma coisa rápida.
Nuno and Miguel are in a rush and want to eat some fast food.

1 14.04 **Listen to the key expressions and repeat each one.**

acho que	*I think that*
uma dose	*a portion*
a fome	*hunger*
e mais nada	*and nothing else*
um refrigerante	*a soft drink*
pedir	*to ask for / order*
para levar	*to take out / away*

2 14.05 **Now listen to the conversation, then answer the questions.**

a Which of the two friends is hungrier, Nuno or Miguel?

Nuno	Então, o que vais escolher?
Miguel	Bom, para mim, acho que quero uma pizza Romana, com uma dose de batatas fritas.
Nuno	Tens muita fome! Eu só quero uma pizza Frango, e mais nada.
Miguel	Não bebes nada?
Nuno	Vou pedir uma Pepsi. E tu, o que queres?
Miguel	Pois, eu também quero um refrigerante. Talvez uma 7-Up.
Nuno	Está bem, então vamos pedir, senão, vamos chegar atrasados ao cinema.
Empregada	Façam favor?
Miguel	É uma pizza Romana com batatas fritas, uma pizza Frango, uma Pepsi e uma 7-Up, se faz favor.
Empregada	É para levar, ou vão comer aqui dentro?
Miguel	É para comer aqui. Obrigado.

b How does Nuno react to what Miguel orders to eat?
c What does Nuno order to drink?
d Where are the boys going after their food?
e Do they eat in, or take the food with them?

1 14.06 **Listen as you look at your snacks and drinks bingo card. You will hear all but one of the items called out in Portuguese. Can you say what it is, in Portuguese?**

milky coffee	custard cake
red wine	chips
orange juice	cheese sandwich

2 **Língua viva – What drinks did the customers who paid this bill have with their meal?**

RESTAURANTE
CAFÉ 𝔉loresta
CERVEJARIA da Cidade

Contribuinte n.º 805 595 570

Travessa Poço da Cidade, 10-12 – 1200 Lisboa
Telef. 346 06 21

TALÃO DE MESA

Couvert	€ 3,25
Aperitivos	2,70
Sopa	
Peixe	
Carne	13,20
Marisco	
Pão	1,00
Vinho	6,45
Águas	1,40
Refrigerantes . . .	
Cerveja	

Listening and reading

1 You will read a blog about some typical national dishes in Portugal. First, listen to some key expressions:

a comida	*food, cuisine*
cada	*each*
os seus próprios	*their own*
as tripas	*tripe*
a carne de porco à Alentejana	*pork and clams Alentejo-style*
a feijoada	*bean and pork stew*
as sardinhas assadas	*grilled sardines*
as sobremesas	*desserts*
o pudim flan	*crême caramel*
os gelados	*ice creams*

2 Now see how much of this food blog you can understand. Listen to it a few times as you read along. Then answer the questions.

> A comida portuguesa é muito variada e deliciosa. Cada região tem os seus próprios pratos típicos como, por exemplo, as tripas no Porto; a carne de porco à Alentejana, no Alentejo; e em Trás-os-Montes, a feijoada. Os portugueses comem muito peixe, como as sardinhas assadas e o bacalhau – dizem que existem 365 receitas para o bacalhau, uma para cada dia do ano! Os portugueses adoram doces e sobremesas como pudim flan, mousse de chocolate, e gelados.

a What do the Portuguese eat a lot of?
b How many recipes are there supposed to be for **bacalhau**?
c What is a typical dish of Porto?
d What is the Portuguese expression for *typical dishes*?
e If **feijoada** is a typical bean and pork stew, what ingredient do you think **feijões** are?

a ementa / a lista

Entradas	*Starters*
Carnes	*Meat*
Peixes	*Fish*
Sobremesas / Doces	*Sweets*
Bebidas	*Drinks*
Vinhos	*Wines*
Couvert	*Cover charge*

pratos do dia

	€
costeletas de porco	6,70
escalopes de peru	7,00
bacalhau à Gomes Sá	7,30
arroz de marisco	11,50/5,90
laranja	0,80
mousse	2,20
pudim	2,40

TIP

Couvert is a *cover charge* for **pão** (*bread*), **manteiga** (*butter*), **azeitonas** (*olives*), etc. You may also be offered **queijo** (*cheese*), **presunto** (*smoked ham*), and **camarões** (*shrimps*). Some of these may come with an extra charge, so establish what you want from the start.

Pratos do dia *Dishes of the day*

Study the menu board – you have a choice of pork chops, turkey steaks, **bacalhau**, or seafood rice. These are usually served with salad, rice and chips. Notice how some dishes have a cheaper price for **uma meia dose** (*a half portion*). As Portuguese portions tend to be huge, this is an option worth considering. For dessert you can have oranges, mousse or crème caramel.

Look at the menu of the day: What is the most economical two-course meal you can order from it? Practise ordering it in Portuguese.

This is usually of average value, but offers a complete meal, with drinks, and means you don't have to spend time on lengthy deliberations.

A ementa turística

Pão e manteiga

carne de porco

ou

pescada

mousse de chocolate

ou

salada de frutas

½ garrafa de vinho /
refrigerante
café

€ 9,70

---

a What main meat course is on offer?

b What can you drink here if you don't like alcohol?

Practice 3

1 Follow the prompts and take part in a conversation with the waiter.

Empregado	Boa noite. Faz favor.
You	**(a)** *Greet the waiter and ask if there is any soup.*
Empregado	Sim, hoje temos sopa de marisco ou caldo verde.
You	**(b)** *Say you'd like a caldo verde.*
Empregado	E depois, para comer?
You	**(c)** *Tell him you'd like a half portion of the cod dish. Ask him if there is salad with it.*
Empregado	Sim, vem com uma pequena salada mista.
You	**(d)** *Say that's OK.*
Empregado	E para sobremesa?
You	**(e)** *Say you'll have the crème caramel.*
Empregado	E para beber?
You	**(f)** *Tell him you'll have half a bottle of white wine and a black coffee afterwards.*

2 14.09 **Now listen and check that your answers are correct.**

3 An inattentive waiter has set out the following menu incorrectly. Where should each item appear? Link up the food and drink (1–14) and the menu sections (A–F).

EMENTA

1 carne de porco à Alentejana

2 pão   A Entradas

3 vinho da casa

4 queijo da Serra

5 manteiga   B Carnes

6 salada de frutas

7 pudim Molotov

8 sopa de legumes   C Sobremesas

9 refrigerantes

10 caldo verde

11 bacalhau à Brás   D Bebidas

12 escalopes de peru

13 pescada

14 água mineral   E Couvert

                            F Peixes

1 What do these words mean?

a um galão
b fresco/a
c uma dose
d mais nada
e caldo verde
f um garoto
g um sumo de laranja
h um refrigerante
i uma imperial
j couvert

2 Complete these phrases by choosing the correct word.

a carne de porco / pescada

b salada de manteiga / frutas

c pastel de nata / galão

d sandes de laranja / fiambre

e sumo de ananás / café

f chá com queijo / limão

g vinho azul / verde

h mousse de chocolate / gelado

i arroz de pudim / mariscos

j sopa de legumes / feijoada

SELF CHECK

	I CAN. . .
○	. . . order food in a café or restaurant
○	. . . recognize typical Portuguese food and drink
○	. . . interpret menus

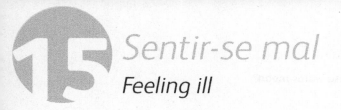

Sentir-se mal
Feeling ill

In this unit you will learn how to:
▶ *talk about minor ailments and remedies.*
▶ *discuss illness.*
▶ *cope with accidents and hospitals.*
▶ *deal with the chemist and doctor.*

CEFR: (A1) *Can ask for or pass on personal details in written form;* **(A2)** *can communicate in simple and routine tasks using simple phrases to ask for and provide things, to get simple information and to discuss what to do next.*

Dealing with health issues

If you do have the misfortune to **ficar doente** (*fall ill*) while in Portugal, and your ailment is only minor, you should go to a **farmácia** (*a chemist's*). Portuguese **farmacêuticos** (*pharmacists*) are usually extremely helpful, and will give advice on most problems so that you may not need to go to see **um médico** (*a doctor*). **Consultas** (*consultations*) with a doctor have to be paid for. You may go to a *local health centre* (**centro de saúde**) or the *hospital* (**o hospital**) if the problem is more serious, but you will not experience problems in being treated – you just need your **cartão europeu de saúde** (*European Health Card, the EHIC*), or your passport. Treatment at **o dentista** (*the dentist*) can be expensive.

On the move, if you are involved, or are **uma testemunha** (*a witness*) to an accident, the national emergency telephone number 112 gets through to all the emergency services, including **os bombeiros** (*firefighters*). You may find the following phrases useful: **Houve um acidente** *There's been an accident*; **Precisamos duma ambulância** *We need an ambulance*; **Precisamos de ajuda** *We need help*.

Can you work out how to say: *we need a doctor?*

Language discovery

Be prepared for dealing with medical problems by learning some of the following basic language. In general, if a part of the body hurts, you say: **dói-me** or **doem-me** (in the plural), plus the part of the body that hurts.

Dói-me a cabeça.	*My head hurts.*
Doem-me os dentes.	*My teeth hurt.*

The breakdown of the structure is: *give(s) pain to me the head (etc.)*.

Note that you do not say *my head hurts*, but simply *the head hurts*. For *sore ears* you say **doem-me os ouvidos**, and not **orelhas** (**orelha** is the outer ear).

You can also say: **Tenho uma dor de** + part of the body = *I have a pain in / on ...*

Tenho uma dor de garganta.	*I have a sore throat.*

Or:

Tenho uma dor em (no, na, nos, nas) + part of the body (lit. *I have a pain in the ...*)

Tenho uma dor nas costas / no pé / na mão ...	*My back / foot / hand hurts.*

If you are reporting on someone else's health, the expressions become:

Dói-lhe ...	*His / her ... hurts.*
Doem-lhe ...	*His / her ... hurt.*

And:

(Ele) tem uma dor ...	*(He) has a pain ...*
(Ela) tem uma dor...	*(She) has a pain ...*

In these circumstances you might well need the names of family members, if you want to say *my husband, son*, etc. and so on. Why not revise Unit 4 now so that you're prepared for the exercises in this unit?

15.01 Listen, and as each part of the body gets mentioned, identify it on the diagram. Then repeat the words.

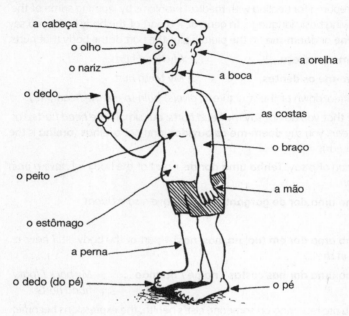

a cabeça
o olho
o nariz
o dedo
o peito
o estômago
a perna
o dedo (do pé)

a orelha
a boca
as costas
o braço
a mão
o pé

Other health problems you might need to report include:

estou constipado/a	*I have a cold*
tenho gripe	*I have flu*
tenho uma insolação	*I have sunstroke*
tenho uma enxaqueca	*I have a migraine*
cortei (cortou) ...	*I've cut (he's/she's cut) ...*
bati (bateu) ...	*I've banged (he's / she's banged) ...*
magoei (magoou) ...	*I've hurt (he's / she's hurt) ...*

15.02 Listen to some examples on the audio and try to repeat each one.

qual é o problema?	*what's the problem?*
o que tem?	*what's the matter?*
onde é que lhe dói?	*where does it hurt?*
estou constipada (f)	*I have a cold*
tenho gripe	*I have flu*
tenho uma insolação	*I have sunstroke*
tenho uma enxaqueca	*I have a migraine*
cortei o dedo	*I've cut my finger*
o meu marido bateu o pé	*my husband has banged his foot*
a minha filha magoou o braço	*my daughter has hurt her arm*

 Notice the absence of the words for *his*, *her* and *my* in the last three expressions. How does Portuguese do it? How do you think you might say *I've hurt my hand*, and *She's cut her leg*?

Diálogo 1

1 15.03 Mr Carvalho feels ill. Listen to the key expressions.

não me sinto bem	*I don't feel well*
sinto-me tonto	*I feel dizzy*
creio que	*I think that*
vomitar	*to be sick / throw up*
não era melhor ... ?	*wouldn't it be better ... ?*
sentar-se	*to sit down*

2 15.04 Now listen to the dialogue. Has Mr Carvalho been sick?

Ana	Bom dia, senhor Carvalho. Como está?
Sr Carvalho	Não me sinto bem.
Ana	Qual é o problema?
Sr Carvalho	Sinto-me tonto e creio que vou vomitar.
Ana	Não era melhor sentar-se um pouco?
Sr Carvalho	Boa ideia. Vou ficar aqui uns momentos.

Practice 1

1 How would you say the following?

  a I have a sore throat.
  b My daughter has cut her finger.
  c My ears hurt.
  d My husband has sunstroke.
  e I think my son is going to be sick.
  f I've banged my toe.
  g My friend has hurt her leg.

2 Would you know how to fill in a form uma ficha (*a form*) like this one? See how much you can do before looking at the word list.

> FICHA DE DADOS PESSOAIS – Centro de Saúde
>
> NOME COMPLETO _____
>
> IDADE _____
>
> DATA DE NASCIMENTO _____
>
> LUGAR DE NASCIMENTO _____
>
> MORADA _____
>
> NÚMERO DE TELEFONE/TELEMÓVEL _____
>
> BILHETE DE IDENTIDADE _____
>
> NÚMERO DE CONTRIBUINTE _____
>
> EM CASO DE EMERGÊNCIA CONTACTAR _____

TIP

o nome completo	*full name*
a idade	*age*
a data de nascimento	*date of birth*
o lugar de nascimento	*place of birth*
a morada	*address*
o número de telefone / telemóvel	*telephone / mobile number*
o bilhete de identidade	*identity card number (or passport for tourists)*
o número de contribuinte	*national insurance number (put personal insurance details if known)*
em caso de emergência, contactar ...	*in case of emergency, contact ...*

Diálogo 2

1 15.05 **Listen first to the key expressions and imitate the speaker.**

tem alguma coisa para ... ?	*do you have something for ...?*
para si, mim	*for you, me*
a criança	*child*
os sintomas	*symptoms*
recomendo	*I recommend*
o xarope	*syrup / cough mixture*
três vezes por dia	*three times a day*
ou	*or*
os comprimidos	*pills*
levo	*I'll take*
de seis em seis horas	*every six hours*

2 15.06 **Now listen to the dialogue. Then answer the questions.**

a What does the chemist want to know from the patient?

Senhora	Tem alguma coisa para dor de garganta?
Farmacêutico	É para si, ou para uma criança?
Senhora	Para mim.
Farmacêutico	Só tem dor de garganta, ou tem outros sintomas também?
Senhora	Tenho uma dorzinha de cabeça também.
Farmacêutico	Bom. Recomendo este xarope para a garganta – tome três vezes por dia. E para a cabeça, estes comprimidos, ou estas aspirinas.
Senhora	Levo os comprimidos.
Farmacêutico	Tome dois de seis em seis horas.

b How often should the lady take the tablets?

Match the following English and Portuguese phrases:

a	comprimidos	1	a bandage
b	uma ligadura	2	ointment for a skin rash
c	um penso rápido	3	a sticking plaster
d	creme para queimaduras solares	4	tablets
e	pomada para uma irritação de pele	5	cream for sunburn

 Practice 2

1 **Língua viva – Look at the information about emergency contacts, and try to answer the questions.**

FARMÁCIAS

LISBOA

Das 22 às 9 horas, chamadas com receitas do dia ou da véspera – 0,30. Chamadas não urgentes – 1,85.

MÉDICO DE URGÊNCIA
☎ 795 06 80

NÚMERO NACIONAL DE SOCORRO

112

VISEU (032)
Bombeiros Municipais – 26216
Bombeiros Voluntários – 26812
Hospital Distrital – 424124
GNR – 421958 e 421585
Brigada de Trânsito – 26637
PSP – 422041
Aeródromo de Viseu – 459849
Electricidade
(Falta de luz e água) – 425175
Serviços Municipalizados – 423112
Rodoviária Beira Litoral – 422822

a What number would you ring if you needed a doctor urgently?

b On the Lisbon pharmacy phone lines, for what do you have to pay 1.85 euros?

c Who do you reach if you dial 112?

d In Viseu, which number would you ring if you wanted the district hospital?

e Why might you ring 424124?

2 15.07 **Listen to five people on the recording saying what is wrong with them, and decide if the following statements are (V) verdadeiro or (F) falso.**

a His leg hurts.
b She has a sore throat.
c His teeth hurt.
d She has sunstroke.
e He's cut his arm.

Test yourself

1 How do you say the following?

    a health centre   **e** I don't feel well.
    b His head hurts.   **f** We need help.
    c arm   **g** Do you have something for ...?
    d I've cut my finger.

2 Margarida can't meet up for coffee. Complete her message with words from the box. Mind you use the correct verb endings.

> não me sinto bem   doer   cortar   garganta   poder
> ter   o médico

Bom dia António!
Desculpa, mas não _____ ir tomar café esta tarde porque
_____. _____ -me a _____ e _____ uma enxaqueca.
Também _____ o braço. Vou ver _____ às 16 horas.
Até à próxima!
Margarida.

Alojamento
Accommodation

In this unit you will learn how to:

▶ *book accommodation in advance.*
▶ *say you have accommodation booked.*
▶ *express problems with your accommodation.*

CEFR: (A2) *Can understand basic types of standard routine correspondence: enquiries, orders, letters of confirmation on familiar topics;* **(A2)** *can discuss everyday practical issues in a simple way when addressed clearly, slowly and directly.*

Places to stay

There is a variety of accommodation available in Portugal, serving the needs and budget of everybody. You could stay in **uma pousada de juventude** (*a youth hostel*) if you are on a budget, or for a bit extra, try **uma pensão** or **uma residencial** (*a guest house*), where you just get **cama e pequeno-almoço** (*bed and breakfast*), or often **só cama** (*bed only*). However, elsewhere, you may be offered **meia-pensão** (*half-board*). Hotels, like everywhere, range from one to five **estrelas** (*stars*). There is also the **estalagem** (*inn*), and for those who want to splash out a little bit more, the now privatized system of **pousadas** – converted castles, monasteries, and stately homes. If you are looking to experience a bit of real Portugal, in the north of the country in particular there is also the option of staying in country houses or farms with a family; known as **turismo de habitação**, or **turismo rural** (*rural tourism*), it's a great way to sample the traditional Portuguese way of life.

Can you work out what might be offered in **a pensão completa?**

1 16.01 **Listen to some of the key vocabulary about hotel rooms.**

um quarto individual	*a single room*
um quarto simples	*a single room*
um quarto duplo com duas camas	*a double room with twin beds*
um quarto de casal	*a double room*
um quarto para família	*a room for a family*
o pequeno-almoço incluído	*breakfast included*

If **cama** means *bed*, and **quarto de casal** means *a double room*, what do you think a **cama de casal** is? You can specify this when booking a room.

Practice 1

1 **Look at the hotel pricing information, and answer the questions.**

Hotel Lusomar

Avenida Praia, Caminha, Minho.
Hotel *** com restaurante, ténis e golfe
28 quartos com ar condicionado, casa de banho completa, telefone, TV.
Preço por dia (pequeno-almoço incluído)

	outubro – março	abril - setembro
quarto individual	€20	€30
quarto duplo	€35	€50
quarto de casal	€40	€60
quarto para família	€60	€80
suite	€65	€90

Suplementos (por pessoa, por dia)

meia-pensão	€10,50
pensão completa	€25
cama extra	€10

What do you think is offered in a **casa de banho completa**? How much do you pay per night for a twin room in high season? Why might you need a **cama extra?**

2 16.02 Listen to the ordinal numbers, including the expression for ground floor, then repeat each expression, concentrating on your pronunciation.

 Diálogo 1

O senhor Green tem um quarto reservado. *Mr Green has a room booked.*

 1 16.03 Listen to the key expressions first, and try to imitate the speaker:

o elevador	*lift*
uma vista bonita	*a lovely view*
o quarto dá para o mar	*the room overlooks the sea*
faça favor de ...	*please ... (+ verb)*
preciso de	*I need*
ficar com	*to keep*

2 16.04 Now listen to the conversation. Before you start, can you remember the Portuguese alphabet? How would you spell out the name *Green*?

Senhor Green	Boa noite. Tenho um quarto reservado para hoje e amanhã.
Rececionista	Em que nome?
Senhor Green	Green. G–R–E–E–N
Rececionista	Aqui está, senhor Green. É o quarto trezentos e vinte e cinco. Fica no terceiro andar; o elevador é ali à direita.
Senhor Green	Tem uma vista bonita?
Rececionista	Tem, sim. O quarto dá para o mar. Faça favor de preencher esta ficha. Preciso de ficar com o seu passaporte.

3 Língua viva – Study the hotel pass, then answer the questions.

Hotel Miraparque

Quarto	311	Preço	€ 36
N.º Pessoas	2	Preço P. Almoço	*GRÁTIS*
Chegada	3/10/14	Partida	11/10/14
Nome	*A. Hills*		

Este cartão servirá para a identificação junto dos serviços do Hotel, que poderão exigir a sua apresentação; conserve este cartão para utilizar no caso de reclamação perante os Serviços Oficiais de Turismo.

AV. SIDÓNIO PAIS, 12 - LISBOA - PORTUGAL - TEL. 57 80 70 - FAX 57 89 20 - TELEX 16745 - MITEL P

---

a How many people was this room for?
b How much extra was breakfast?

Go further

1 Complete the email booking rooms at a hotel using words from the box. Then answer the questions.

quarto de casal   quarto   reservar   completa   abril   extra
noites   individuais   maio   3 anos

Estimados senhores,

Gostaria de _____ quartos em nome de Brown, pensão _____:
um _____, com cama _____ para uma criança de _____
dois quartos _____
um _____ de família
É para 10 _____, do dia 26 de _____ ao 6 de _____. Somos
9 pessoas.

Aguardo a vossa resposta,

Com os meus cumprimentos

Atenciosamente

Sally Brown (senhora)

---

aguardo a vossa resposta	*I look forward to your reply*
com os meus cumprimentos	*with my compliments*
atenciosamente	*yours sincerely / faithfully*

a How many single rooms does Mrs Brown want?
b How many people are there in her group?
c What is their departure date?
d What do you think **estimados** means?

2 Now read the response from the hotel, then answer the questions:

Estimada senhora Brown,

Venho por estes meios confirmar a reserva, para 10 noites, para o grupo de 9 pessoas, para o dia 26 de abril. A nossa receção abre 24 horas, mas para chegadas depois das 22.00, é favor telefonar com antecedência.

O preço total para a visita é 1,750 euros; sem cobrar a criança de 3 anos.

Precisamos dos detalhes do cartão de crédito para fazer a reserva.

Sem mais assunto de momento, subscrevo-me

Atenciosamente

José Fernandes

Hotel Lusomar

venho por estes meios	*I would like to (lit. I come through these means)*
a nossa receção	*our reception*
chegadas depois das 22.00 h	*arrivals after 10 p.m.*
com antecedência	*beforehand / in advance*
sem cobrar	*without charging*
sem mais assunto de momento	*without anything else at the moment*
subscrevo-me	*yours (lit. I sign myself)*

a Which word suggests that the hotel is able to accommodate Mrs Brown's reservation?

b What do they have to do if they are arriving after 10 p.m.?

c How much is being charged for the small child?

d What information does the hotel need to confirm the reservation?

Diálogo 2

QUANDO AS COISAS NÃO FUNCIONAM ... *WHEN THINGS DON'T WORK ...*

1 16.05 **Listen to the key expressions first.**

o aquecimento	the heating
não está a funcionar bem	isn't working well
mandar	to send
alguém	someone
dar uma vista de olhos	to have a look
peço desculpa	I'm sorry
como vê	as you can see
o ascensor	lift
por causa de	because of
o corte de eletricidade	power cut
ontem à noite	last night
arranjar	to arrange, sort out

2 16.06 **Now listen to the conversation in the hotel reception. What is wrong with Laura's room?**

Laura	Desculpe, o aquecimento no quarto não está a funcionar bem.
Rececionista	Qual é o número do quarto?
Laura	É o duzentos e quinze. É possível mandar alguém vir dar uma vista de olhos?
Rececionista	Claro. Peço desculpa. Como vê, o ascensor também está avariado. Creio que é por causa do corte de eletricidade ontem à noite. Vou ver se podemos arranjar qualquer coisa, está bem?
Laura	Obrigada.

Language discovery

TALKING ABOUT WHAT'S HAPPENING NOW

Estar in the present tense + **a** + verb, is used to describe an action which is ongoing or takes place at the time of speaking. You can use this construction with any verb:

estou a falar	*I am speaking (now)*
estamos a pensar	*we are thinking*
Maria está a estudar chinês.	*Mary is studying Chinese (at the moment).*
Eles estão a jogar golfe.	*They are playing golf.*

 Practice 2

1 **Can you match up the Portuguese and English statements about things that are not working properly?**

a O elevador está avariado.

b A água não está a funcionar.

c O fogão não funciona.

d A fechadura não está a funcionar bem.

e O ar condicionado está avariado.

1 The cooker doesn't work.

2 The lift has broken down.

3 The lock isn't working well.

4 The water isn't working.

5 The air-conditioning has broken down.

2 **You arrive at a hotel. Follow the prompts to take part in a dialogue with the receptionist.**

You	**(a)** *Say good morning. Say you have a room booked for three nights.*
Rececionista	Em que nome?
You	**(b)** *Say 'Graves' and spell it.*
Rececionista	Aqui está. É o quarto vinte e sete. Fica no segundo andar.
You	**(c)** *Ask if it has air-conditioning.*
Rececionista	Tem, sim. Todos os quartos têm.
You	**(d)** *Ask if it has a nice view.*
Rececionista	Tem, sim – o quarto dá para as montanhas.
You	**(e)** *Say thank you.*

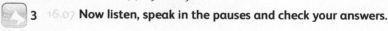 3 16.07 **Now listen, speak in the pauses and check your answers.**

4 **How much of the alphabet can you remember? Listen to some celebrities spelling out their names. Try to write down what you hear and listen to confirm that you are correct.**

You can go back to the Pronunciation guide and review the introductory section. Then, practise spelling out your own name.

Test yourself

1 Give the English for:
 a somos quatro
 b um quarto para família
 c lamento
 d obrigada pela ajuda
 e uma pensão
 f com casa de banho
 g um quarto duplo
 h com cama de casal
 i o quarto dá para as montanhas
 j uma ficha

2 Match both halves of the sentences to complete a hotel satisfaction survey.

a A comida no restaurante	1 não funcionam bem.
b Os preços do hotel	2 muito limpos.
c Os ascensores	3 excelentes.
d Os desportos são	4 é deliciosa.
e Os quartos estão	5 são um pouco caros.

SELF CHECK

I CAN. . .
. . . book accommodation in advance
. . . say I have accommodation booked
. . . express problems with hotel accommodation

Divertimentos
Distractions

In this unit you will learn how to:
▶ *talk about outdoor activities.*
▶ *talk about cultural activities.*
▶ *discuss the weather.*
▶ *express a basic action in the past.*

CEFR: (A2) *Can ask and answer questions about pastimes and past activities;* **(A2)** *can discuss what to do in the evening, at the weekend.*

Enjoying life in Portugal

There are many things to see and do in Portugal. For example, you can visit some of the loveliest and oldest **castelos** (*castles*) and **palácios** (*palaces*) in Europe. Religious buildings are magnificent, from **mosteiros** (*monasteries*) to **conventos** (*convents*), **igrejas** (*churches*) and **catedrais** (*cathedrals*). **A natureza** (*nature*) features highly as a prized attraction, with many areas of outstanding natural beauty including **parques nacionais** (*national parks*), **florestas** (*forests*), and **serras** (*mountain ranges*). There are plenty of culture-rich **museus** (*museums*) and **galerias de arte** (*art galleries*) to visit too, and **monumentos** (*monuments*) round every corner.

You can participate in **desportos** (*sport*); **ténis** (*tennis*), **golfe** (*golf*), **futebol** (*football*), **voleibol** (*volleyball*), and down on the **praia** (*beach*) **desportos aquáticos** (*water sports*) are popular, especially (**fazer surf**) *surfing*. Or you can simply **passear** (*go for a stroll*), sit at an outdoor café, read a paper, sip a cooling drink, and **ver o mundo passar** (*watch the world go by*). **Perfeito!**

What might you expect to find in a **museu de arte moderna?**
What activity do you think **vólei de praia** is?

Diálogo 1

Jorge e Teresa decidem-se a ir à praia. *Jorge and Teresa decide to go to the beach.*

1 17.01 **Listen to the key expressions and imitate the speaker.**

é ideal para	*it's ideal for*
podemos	*we can*
a tarde inteira	*the whole afternoon*
que tal?	*how about it?*
sozinho	*alone*
preguiçosa (f)	*lazy*
cuidado	*careful*
é perigoso	*it's dangerous*
a proteção	*protection*

2 17.02 **Now listen to the dialogue. What does Jorge suggest they play at the beach?**

Jorge	Vamos à praia hoje?
Teresa	Está bem. Faz calor, é ideal para ir nadar. Podemos levar um piquenique, e passar a tarde inteira. Que tal?
Jorge	Boa! Podemos jogar voleibol.
Teresa	Tu podes jogar sozinho; eu quero apanhar o sol e dormir!
Jorge	Preguiçosa! Cuidado com o sol. É perigoso dormir. Precisamos de levar proteção contra o sol.

3 **Can you find the missing Portuguese words from the text?**

faz _____	*it's hot*
levar	*to take*
um _____	*a picnic*
boa!	*great idea!*
apanhar o _____	*to sunbathe*
dormir	*to sleep*
_____	*against*

 Diálogo 2

O Senhor Mendes e a Senhora Oliveira falam sobre o que fizeram ontem.
Mr Mendes and Mrs Oliveira talk about what they did yesterday.

1 17.03 **First listen to the key expressions.**

o que fez ontem?	*what did you (sing.) do yesterday?*
o que fizeram lá?	*what did you (pl.) do there?*
levámos	*we took*
andámos	*we walked*
vimos	*we saw*
tantas borboletas	*so many butterflies*
trabalhei	*I worked*

2 17.04 **Now listen to the dialogue, then answer the questions.**

a What did Mrs Oliveira and her family take to the park?

Senhor Mendes	O que fez ontem?
Senhora Oliveira	Ontem, pois, fui com a minha família ao parque.
Senhor Mendes	O que fizeram lá?
Senhora Oliveira	Levámos um piquenique, e andámos à sombra das árvores. Os meus filhos jogaram futebol, e vimos muitas coisas – pássaros, flores, e tantas borboletas!
Senhor Mendes	Foram ao lago também?
Senhora Oliveira	Fomos. E o senhor, fez alguma coisa interessante?
Senhor Mendes	Eu? Trabalhei o dia inteiro!

b What did they see in the park?
c What did Sr Mendes do?

o parque	*park*
à sombra das árvores	*in the shade of the trees*
jogaram	*(they) played*
os pássaros	*birds*
as flores	*flowers*
o lago	*lake*

 Sra Oliveira uses **fui** to say *I went*. How does Sr Mendes ask *Did you all go to the lake*? How does Sra Oliveira reply *Yes, we did go*?

Language discovery

Here are the past tense verb endings for the three regular groups **-ar**, **-er**, **-ir**. Use the simple past tense to talk about completed actions, such as **falei com a Ana** *I spoke with Ana*, **comemos um bolo** *we ate a cake*, **partiram às três horas** *they left at 3 o'clock*.

	falar to speak	comer to eat	partir to leave
eu	falei	comi	parti
tu	falaste	comeste	partiste
ele, ela, você	falou	comeu	partiu
nós	falámos	comemos	partimos
eles, elas, vocês	falaram	comeram	partiram

How would you say *You* (**tu**) *bought* (**comprar**) *the cakes.* What about *I drank* (**beber**) *the wine*?

Here are three of the most common irregular verbs you need to know. You would say **vi um filme interessante** *I saw an interesting film*, **ela fez as compras** *she did the shopping*, **fomos à praia** *we went to the beach*.

	ir to go	fazer to do, make	ver to see
eu	fui	fiz	vi
tu	foste	fizeste	viste
ele, ela, você	foi	fez	viu
nós	fomos	fizemos	vimos
eles, elas, vocês	foram	fizeram	viram

Look back at the dialogue: how many past tense forms of **ir** can you find?

These common expressions are useful when referring to past events.

ontem	*yesterday*
anteontem	*the day before yesterday*
a semana passada	*last week*
o mês passado	*last month*
o ano passado	*last year*
a quinta (feira) passada	*last Thursday*
nas férias passadas	*last holiday*
ontem à noite	*last night*

 Practice 1

1 **To make five complete sentences in the past, link the words from each column.**

a	O Paulo	viste	ao parque.
b	Tu	fizeram	o filme.
c	Eu e a Maria	foi	ontem.
d	Vocês	visitámos	muitas coisas interessantes.
e	Eu	trabalhei	a cidade.

2 **Supply these past-tense sentences using the verbs suggested.**

a Yesterday we played (**jogar**) volleyball.

b Last week I visited (**visitar**) the castle.

c Last year John stayed (**ficar**) in the forest.

d Last Saturday they slept (**dormir**) on the beach.

e Last night you (**tu**) made (**fazer**) a cake.

f The day before yesterday Ana lost (**perder**) her (the) mobile phone.

Language discovery

	Hoje *Today*	Amanhã *Tomorrow*
	Faz sol. **Há sol.** *It's sunny.*	**Vai fazer sol. / Vai haver sol.** *It's going to be sunny.*
	Faz calor. **Está calor** (colloq.) **Está quente.** *It's hot.*	**Vai fazer calor.** **Vai estar calor.** **Vai estar quente.** *It's going to be hot.*
	Faz vento. **Há vento.** *It's windy.*	**Vai fazer vento.** **Vai haver vento.** *It's going to be windy.*
	Está a chover. *It's raining.*	**Vai chover.** *It's going to rain.*
	Faz frio. **Está frio.** *It's cold.*	**Vai fazer frio.** **Vai estar frio.** *It's going to be cold.*
	Está a nevar. **Há neve.** *It's snowing.*	**Vai nevar.** **Vai haver neve.** *It's going to snow.*

i Practice 2

1 Match up these captions with the appropriate weather symbols.

a Faz frio.   1

b Há neve.   2

c Há sol.   3

d Está a chover.   4

e Faz vento.   5

2 17.05 **Listen to the weather forecasts for four cities around the Portuguese-speaking world, and choose the correct word to complete each statement. You will hear the answers on the audio.**

1 Today, in Lisbon, the wind is …
  a strong   **b** light

2 In Rio it's …
  a very hot   **b** warm

3 Tomorrow in Maputo, the capital of Mozambique, the sky is going to be …
  a clear   **b** slightly cloudy

4 In Luanda, the capital of Angola, it's going to …
  a be sunny   **b** rain

Reading

Read the leaflet about the range of activities available in the Algarve. Focus on the key words in each paragraph to get a general understanding.

Região de turismo do Algarve

1 MERCADOS

Tudo se compra, tudo se vende. Desde a fresca hortaliça às flores perfumadas. E, também, fruta, objectos de uso diário, vestuário, etc.

2 EXPOSIÇÕES

Conhecer as obras de artistas portugueses e estrangeiros. Uma forma de enriquecer as suas férias.

3 FOLCLORE

A dança algarvia, é alegre, rápida. Fala de dias de sol, de tradições que são eternas. E a sua música fica no ouvido...

4 PARQUES DE DIVERSÕES

A alegria e o sol juntam-se para horas de prazer, de puro divertimento. Uma forma sempre agradável de ver dias de férias com toda a família.

5 ATIVIDADES CULTURAIS

Passeio à descoberta do património natural e arqueológico desta zona do interior rural do concelho de Portimão.

6 FADO

Ouvir o fado é penetrar os segredos da alma portuguesa. Nos sons plangentes da guitarra, Fado é alegria e tristeza, é música que se ouve em silêncio, é uma recordação que fica para sempre.

Your family members all like different things. Look at their interests, then decide which activity or venue is most likely to please each person.

Mother — Likes looking at paintings. Wants to do something cultural, but prefers to be inside.

Father — Is keen on the outdoor life, and has an interest in old ruins, and areas of natural beauty.

Two young sisters — Want to do an activity involving all the family.

Grandparents — Prefer something a bit less energetic. Grandad is an enthusiastic guitar player.

Practice 3

1 Complete the sentences with the correct past tense form of the verbs in brackets.

a Ontem eu _____ (ir) à praia.

b Nas férias passadas Emily _____ (visitar) um museu.

c O ano passado nós _____ (ver) muitos pássaros nas montanhas.

d A semana passada John e Edward _____ (ir) a um castelo.

e Tu _____ (jogar) golfe anteontem?

f Vocês _____ (fazer) surf o domingo passado?

2 17.06 **Listen to Ana talking about what she did this past week. Then answer the questions. You will hear the answers on the audio.**

a What did Ana do with her family in Évora?

b What did she buy on Saturday?

c What did her friend eat in the new restaurant?

d At what time did Ana arrive home from work yesterday?

e What did she do before going to bed?

3 **Take part in the conversation by following the English prompts.**

Barbara	O que fez a semana passada?
You	**(a)** *Say that last week you and your sister visited Lisbon.*
Barbara	O que fizeram lá?
You	**(b)** *Say that you went to a palace, and saw many interesting things.*
Barbara	Levaram um piquenique?
You	**(c)** *Say no, we ate in a café in the square.*
Barbara	Gostaram da visita?
You	**(d)** *Say that you both enjoyed it very much.*

4 17.07 **Listen again to the key expressions and confirm your answers.**

5 Read Mariana's blog about her visit to Brazil, then supply the questions to ask her more about it.

Olá amigos!

Visita da Mariana ao Brasil ...

O ano passado fui ao Brasil. Passei dez dias lá, e visitei o Rio de Janeiro, Salvador e Ouro Preto. Comi feijoada brasileira e muitas frutas tropicais. Jogámos vólei de praia e vários desportos aquáticos. Adorei!

Tchau!

6 Now, you want to find out more about Mariana's trip. Post an entry on her blog, asking in Portuguese:

Olá _____

Eu quero saber _____ (visitar / Brasília?). Que comida típica _____ (comer?). _____ (ir a floresta?) _____ Como é o norte do Brasil, _____ (fazer calor?)

Eu também _____ (gostar / desportos)

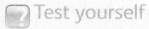

1 Can you work out the meaning of these words and expressions?

a nadar
b parque
c ela falou
d a semana passada
e floresta
f folclore
g piquenique
h à sombra
i eu fui
j a segunda-feira passada

2 Match up the English and Portuguese past time expressions.

a anteontem   1 in the last holidays
b a quarta-feira passada   2 last night
c nas férias passadas   3 the day before yesterday
d o mês passado   4 last year
e o sábado passado   5 last Saturday
f ontem   6 yesterday
g ontem à noite   7 last Wednesday
h o ano passado   8 last month

SELF CHECK

I CAN...
...talk about outdoor activities
...talk about cultural activities
...discuss the weather
...express a basic action in the past

Key to the exercises

UNIT 1

Culture The missing words are: morning / evening (night) / bye (ciao!) / goodbye

Diálogo 1 2 it's morning, **4** adeus (goodbye), até logo (see you later)

Language discovery The difference is a degree of politeness and familiarity.

Practice 1 1 está / Estou / bem, obrigada / noite / até / Boa, **2 a** Olá, bom dia. **b** Bom dia or boa tarde (if after midday). **c** Boa tarde, até amanhã. **d** Adeus (or Tchau), até logo / até já. **e** Olá, boa noite. **3 Língua viva:** morning (todas as manhãs)

Diálogo 2 2 a Miguel, **b** Estás boa?

Practice 2 1 a Boa tarde, estou bem obrigado/a. E o Nuno, como está? **b** Adeus (tchau), até amanhã. **3 a** Como se chama? **b** Como te chamas? **c** Como se chama (o senhor)? **4** Bom dia, como está? / Estou bem, obrigado, e a senhora? / Bem, obrigada. / Desculpe, como se chama? / Chamo-me Lúcia, e o senhor? / Eduardo. / Muito prazer. / Igualmente.

Test yourself 1 a 3, **b** 5, **c** 1, **d** 6, **e** 4, **f** 2, **2 a** próxima, **b** bem, **c** Como, **d** o, **e** chama, **f** me, **g** muito, **h** faz

UNIT 2

Culture train / bus / sport

Diálogo 1 a Lisbon (Lisboa), **b** Londres

Language discovery Ser is used for more permanent situations and **estar** for situations of a temporary nature.

Practice 1 1 a 6, **b** 3, **c** 1, **d** 4, **e** 7, **f** 2, **g** 5, **2 a** portuguesa, **b** Alemanha, **c** americanas, **d** ingleses, **e** Itália, **f** escocês. **3 b** Os senhores Schmidt são alemães. Eles são da Alemanha. **c** A Ellen e a Mary são dos Estados Unidos. Elas são americanas. **d** A Sandra, o John e a Brenda são da Inglaterra. Eles são ingleses. **e** O Marco Giovanni é italiano. Ele é da Itália. **f** O Mac é da Escócia. Ele é escocês.

Diálogo 2 **2** Brazilian

Practice 2 **1 a** Fala italiano? **b** Não sou americano/a. **c** Falo português
e inglês. **d** Fala português? **e** Não sou alemão/ã, mas falo alemão.
2 a F, **b** V, **c** V, **d** V, **e** F, **3 Língua viva**: **a** English, **b** German, Italian.
4 a Sim, falo um pouco. **b** Não, não sou alemão/ã, sou (inglês/a).
c Sim, falo inglês e (também) italiano. **d** Obrigado/a, adeus.
5 English, Portuguese, German. **6 a** evening **b** Barcelona **c** sou / são /
somos, **7 a** bom dia, **b** é, **c** sou, **d** grega, **e** de onde é, **f** portuguesa, **g** de

Test yourself **1 a** De onde é, Paulo? **b** Sou da (Inglaterra). **c** (o senhor
Mendes) é brasileiro? **d** De onde são? **e** Somos (ingleses / inglesas). **f** A
Júlia é portuguesa. **g** O João é dos Estados Unidos? **h** Fala inglês? **i** Não,
não falo alemão. **j** Sim, sou inglês / inglesa. **2 a** a, **b** a, **c** o, **d** o, **e** os,
f as, **g** ✓, **h** o, **3 a** brasileiros, **b** espanhóis, **c** alemã, **d** grego, **e** chinesas,
f franceses

UNIT 3

Culture **a** 5th October Avenue, No. 25, 3rd floor on right, Lisbon, **b** avenue
name, building number, floor number, left or right side apartment, city

Diálogo 1 **2** in Brazil

Language discovery as ruas, os dias, as senhoras

Language discovery feminine, masculine/plural

Practice 1 **1 a** mora na, **b** moramos na, **c** moro em, **d** moram na, **e** moras
em, **2 a** Onde mora (vive) Senhora Gomes? **b** Moro (vivo) na Inglaterra.
c A Maria mora (vive) na praça. **d** Onde moram os senhores? **e** (O Renato)
vive na Alemanha?

Listening and reading **2 a** Silves, Algarve, **b** Samora Barros Street, **c** 3rd
floor, on the left, **4 a** Lisboa (Lisbon), **b** on a square (Praça de Camões)

Language discovery because casa (house) is feminine; a primeira praça

Language discovery masculine / duas casas antigas

Practice 2 **1 Língua viva**: Pastelaria Antiqua, **2 a** 3, **b** 4, **c** 1, **d** 2, **e** 5

Diálogo 2 **2 a** Maria works in the airport in Faro, at check-in. **b** Paulo is a
banker.

Practice 3 **1 a** Onde trabalha senhor Gomes? **b** Sou estudante. **c** O que faz, José? **d** Trabalho num/a … **e** Não trabalho. **2 a** cinco, **b** doze, **c** treze, **d** dezoito, **e** dois, **f** dezanove, **3 a** 4, **b** 6, **c** 1, **d** 3, **e** 2, **f** 5

Test yourself **1 a** Trabalho numa escola. **b** Onde moram os senhores? **c** Moro na praça. **d** Ela é professora. **e** Moramos numa casa moderna. **f** Onde trabalha? **g** O que faz? **2 a** no, **b** na, **c** numa, **d** num, **e** na, **f** no, **3** (typical responses) **a** Chamo-me Edith Ward, **b** Moro em Preston, **c** Sou professora **d** Trabalho numa escola.

UNIT 4

Culture Tenho dezoito anos.

Diálogo 1 **2** you can also say esposa

Practice 1 **1 a** o meu irmão. **b** a nossa mãe. **c** a sua filha. **d** os nossos filhos. **e** o meu pai. **2 a** A Ana é a filha mais nova. **b** O Miguel é o nosso irmão mais alto. **c** Eles são os meus filhos mais velhos. **d** o António é mais baixo. **e** a Maria e a Paula são mais altas.

Listening and reading **2** three, **3 a** Chama-se Rosa. **b** Trabalha numa escola secundária. **c** É o Roberto. **d** É muito calma. **e** Trabalha num hospital. **f** Não, é alto.

Language discovery tem / Tem filhos?

Language discovery arrogant / timid (shy) / serious / cheerful / artistic / honest

Practice 2 **1 a** Tem uma filha? **b** Temos dois filhos. **c** Ela tem um irmão? **d** Tenho uma irmã. **e** Têm filhos? **2** Preguiçoso, elegante, desportivo, barulhento, sério, calmo, nervoso, honesto, **3 Língua viva**: age up to 25, not a student, artistic

Diálogo 2 **2** she is 20

Practice 3 **1 a** este, **b** aquela, **c** estas, **d** esta, **e** aqueles, **2 a** F, **b** F, **c** T, **d** F, **e** T

Test yourself **1 a** 8, **b** 6, **c** 1, **d** 4, **e** 7, **f** 2, **g** 5, **h** 3, **2 a** está, **b** correct, **c** tem, **d** são, **e** correct, **f** correct

Culture a senhora / tu

Diálogo **2** She likes them but not a lot as they are very salty. **3** sardines / I like / salt

Language discovery ele mora, (eu) gosto, elas trabalham

Language discovery Gostamos muito / Gosto, mas não muito

Practice 1 **1 a** Os senhores Brito gostam de frango? **b** Não gostas do caldo verde? **c** Não, não gosto. **d** Gostamos muito (imenso) de sardinhas. **e** a Paula gosta um pouco de arroz de marisco. **f** Gostam imenso da comida portuguesa. **2 a** -a, **b** -o, **c** -amos, **d** -as, **e** -am. **3 a** 3, **b** 1, **c** 5, **d** 2, **e** 4. **4 Língua viva**: seafood rice (arroz de marisco).

Listening and reading **3** Switzerland / Denmark / Japan / Netherlands

Practice 2 **4 a** Sim. Gosta. **b** Porque é um país muito limpo. **c** Porque tem um clima agradável. **d** Não, não gostam muito. **e** a mulher do Nuno. **f** Porque preferem o barulho.

Language discovery unpleasant / modern / historical / interesting / cultural

Practice 3 **1 a** barulhento, **b** modernas, **c** histórica, **d** barata, **e** interessantes, **2 a** Prefiro / cultural, **b** Gostamos de / bonito, **c** Gostam da / comida italiana, **d** Não gosto do / Japão, **3** Língua viva: Something different. **5** 1 movimentado, 2 desagradável, 3 sujo, 4 barato, 5 caro, 6 agradável, 7 velho, 8 calmo, 9 moderno, 10 limpo, **6 a** ele pinta, **b** nós conversamos, **c** eu canto, **d** a Mary limpa a casa, **e** Os senhores cantam?, **f** Tu pintas?

Test yourself **1 a** Gosta de frango? **b** Gosto um pouco de sardinhas. **c** O Miguel gosta imenso da comida portuguesa. **d** O Senhor não gosta do caldo verde? **e** Prefiro Portugal porque é interessante. **f** Qual preferem – a Itália ou o Japão? **g** Preferimos a comida dinamarquesa. **2 a** 2, **b** 1, **c** 5, **d** 6, **e** 3, **f** 4

Culture the living room / lounge, the kitchen, the garage

Listening and reading **1 2** in an apartment, **3 a** 3, **b** 5, **c** 2, **d** 4, **e** 1

Esta é a única coisa de que não gosto. / Esta é a única coisa de que gosto.

Diálogo 2 a three, **b** it's quite large, **c** living room, dining room, large kitchen, **d** she likes it a lot

Practice 1 1 típica / três / pequenos / grande / terraço / há / casa de banho / baixo / cozinha / de / sala de jantar. **2** (sample answer) A minha casa é uma casa moderna. Fica num bairro moderno. Na casa há dois quartos em cima, e uma cozinha e uma sala de estar em baixo. Gosto da minha casa. **3 a** baixo, **b** grande, **c** há, **d** estar, **e** sala

Listening and reading 2 2 frigorífico, **3 a** sofa / a vase of flowers / the cat / a wardrobe, cupboard, **4 a** Em frente da lareira. **b** Um vaso de flores. **c** Debaixo da mesa. **d** Sim, há. **e** Um quadro bonito e um armário. **f** Não; há um chuveiro.

Go further em cima da mesa / em frente do sofá

Practice 2 1 a F, **b** F, **c** F, **d** V, **e** F, **f** V, **2 a** O gato está em cima do frigorífico. **b** Há um armário ao lado da estante. **c** Há um sofá detrás da mesa? **d** O chuveiro não está na cozinha. **e** O fogão está ao lado da máquina de lavar. **f** O gato está em frente da poltrona? **3 Língua viva: a** three, **b** yes, **4 a** verdadeiro, **b** verdadeiro, **c** verdadeiro, **d** falso, **e** falso, **5** moderno / Lisboa / quinto andar / alto / tem / dois / uma sala / cozinha, **6 a** 3, **b** 5, **c** 1, **d** 4, **e** 2

Test yourself 1 a Tenho um apartamento. **b** A minha casa tem três quartos. **c** Como é a sua casa? **d** Tenho uma cozinha grande. **e** Há duas casas de banho. **f** Não há uma sala de jantar. **g** O sofá está ao lado da mesa. **h** O frigorífico está na cozinha. **i** O que há na sala de estar? **2 a** 4, **b** 6, **c** 1, **d** 3, **e** 5, **f** 2

UNIT 7

Culture almoço

Listening and reading 2 a get dressed, **b** leave work, **c** she goes to an English lesson.

Language discovery Chego ao escritório.
4 a 4, **b** 1, **c** 2, **d** 5, **e** 3

Language discovery (ela) deita-se

Language discovery (Ele) tem vinte e um anos.

Practice 1 1 answers on the audio, 2 **a** levanta-se, **b** 9 horas, **c** janta / sete menos um quarto, **d** aula de japonês, **e** à uma. **3 a** 3, **b** 6, **c** 4, **d** 1, **e** 5, **f** 2, **4** (Sample answers) **a** Levanto-me às 7 horas. **b** Almoço ao meio-dia. **c** Chego em casa às 5 e meia. **d** Deito-me às 10 e um quarto. **5 a** 3, **b** 1, **c** 4, **d** 2, **e** 5.

Diálogo 1 **2** jantamos, **3** jogar / come, **4 a** 8.30 a.m. **b** he plays football, **c** she attends church

Language discovery Como se chama?

Language discovery the nós-person is different – comemos and partimos

Practice 2 1 **Língua viva:** Wednesday a.m. (4a feira de manhã) **2 a** Levanto-me cedo. **b** Ele não se deita tarde. **c** A que horas se vestem? **d** Não nos vestimos rapidamente. **e** Como se chamam? **f** A que horas te levantas? **3a** compreende, **b** parte, **c** comemos, **d** vivem, **e** abres, **f** bebe. **4 a** ao, **b** às, **c** a, **d** à, **e** a, **f** aos

Diálogo 2 **2** it's five minutes to two

Test yourself 1 **a** A que horas se levanta? **b** Não nos deitamos até às 10 e meia. **c** A que horas almoça nos / aos domingos (Paulo)? **d** Não como muito nas / às terças. **e** A que horas vai à igreja Jorge? **f** Que horas são? **2 a** vinte e quatro, **b** setenta, **c** noventa, **d** sessenta e dois, **e** cento e um, **3** the correct order is: c / e / a / f / b / d

UNIT 8

Culture a música jazz / gosto do teatro

Diálogo 1 **2 a** adoro, **b** José, **c** Brazilian soap operas, **d** Adoro ouvir música. **3** pergunta / música / pintar / passear no / ver

Language discovery (eles) gostam de ler / the meaning is really the same: What is it that you like doing?, What do you like doing?

Practice 1 1 **a** Maria, o que gosta de fazer no tempo livre? **b** Gosto de mergulhar. **c** Os senhores gostam de viajar? **d** Gostam de praticar desportos? **e** Não gosto de trabalhar no jardim. **f** Gostas de nadar no tempo livre? **2 a** Sim, claro. **b** Não, não somos portugueses, somos ingleses. Somos de … **c** Sim, falo um pouco de português. **d** Gosto de ir ao teatro. **e** O meu marido / a minha mulher gosta de trabalhar no jardim,

e os meus filhos gostam de praticar desportos. **f** Sim, claro! **4 Língua viva**:
Casa do Brasil

Language discovery swimming

Listening and reading **2** jazz, **4** every day, for at least an hour, **5 a** read,
b often (many times), **c** surf the Web and watch TV, **d** Nuno

Practice 2 **1** livros / leio / dias / vejo / ouve / joga / nunca / lê / gosta / vão
/ todas / vez / quando / fazem. **2 a** 3, **b** 6, **c** 4, **d** 1, **e** 5, **f** 2. **3 a** ouço, **b** lês,
c vê, **d** fazemos, **e** ouvir, **4 Língua viva**: every day, **5 1** c, **2** a, **3** b, **4** a

Test yourself **1 a** O que gosta de fazer no tempo livre? **b** Gosto de
(dançar, etc.) **c** Claro que pode. **d** Vejo a televisão (todos os dias, etc.)
e Ouvem muitas vezes a música? **f** Vou à cidade para fazer compras.
2 a 3, **b** 6, **c** 4, **d** 1, **e** 5, **f** 2

UNIT 9

Culture Gosto de tirar férias ao estrangeiro / They are not from round
here (from this land).

Diálogo 1 **2 a** Greece, **b** foreign food, **c** his children are not going with
him, **3** Greece / culture / France

Language discovery through, by the sea / through, along the streets

Language discovery pela avenida / pelo parque / pelas praias

Practice 1 **1 a** Vou muitas vezes para a Itália na primavera. **b** Gosto da
cultura italiana. **c** O nosso filho sempre vem connosco, mas a nossa filha
prefere viajar com o namorado. **d** Em geral ficamos em casa, mas eu e a
minha família queremos conhecer a França no outono. **2** answers on the
audio, **3 a** sei, **b** conhece, **c** sabem, **d** conhecem, **e** sei, **f** sabemos.

Diálogo 2 **2 a** Spain, November, **b** India / she doesn't have much money,
3 a 3, **b** 1, **c** 4, **d** 2

Language discovery spring (a primavera)

Language discovery (ele) Gostaria de pintar a casa / (Eu) Gostaria de
viajar pelo mar.

Practice 2 **1** (possible answers) **a** Eu vou tirar férias em abril. **b** Tu vais viajar
pela Escócia no ano que vem. **c** Você vai visitar o meu amigo amanhã. **d**
Nós vamos trabalhar no jardim no sábado. **e** Os senhores vão nadar no
mar em julho. **f** Eles vão jogar golfe na sexta-feira. **2 a** Gostaria de visitar a
Alemanha. **b** O Paulo não gostaria de trabalhar na segunda-feira.

c Gostariam de beber connosco? **d** O meu marido / a minha mulher gostaria de provar a comida brasileira. **e** Gostaríamos de viajar pelos Estados Unidos. **3 Língua viva:** end June–September

Practice 3 **1** answers on the audio, **2 a** C, **b** I, **c** I, **d** C, **e** C.

Test yourself **1 a** Onde vão passar as férias este ano? **b** Quero conhecer a Grécia. **c** A minha família sempre passa as férias em Portugal. **d** Sabe nadar? **e** (e.g.) No ano que vem vou passar as férias na Itália. **f** Quer vir também? **2 a** março, **b** junho, **c** setembro, **d** dezembro, **e** abril, **f** inverno, **g** outono, **h** verão

UNIT 10

Culture livrinho / casa / jogão

Diálogo 1 **2 a** no, **b** no, she's going to the dentist first, **c** on foot

Diálogo 2 **2 a** todos os dias, **b** it's fast and cheap, **c** coach, plane

Language discovery de comboio / vou de camioneta, vou de avião

Language discovery **1 a** 4, **b** 5, **c** 6, **d** 1, **e** 7, **f** 8, **g** 9, **h** 2, **i** 3

Practice 1 **1** geral / de / volto / dias / barato / rápido / fins / fora / vou / gosto / bicicleta / férias / barco / avião. **2** 862 / 1,241 / 349 / 2,766 / 299 / 758 / 5,512 / 10,150 / 683 / 3,371, **3 Língua viva:** 23747 / 29624. **4 a** a bicycle, **b** 20 euros, **c** either of: arrive more quickly at work, improve your health

Go further Pode-se alugar bicicletas aqui? / the -ar verbs change to an -e ending and the -er and -ir verbs change the other way, to an -a

Practice 2 **1 a** Vou ao trabalho no carro do meu amigo (da minha amiga). **b** O Paulo vai ao hospital de autocarro. **c** A Ana viaja no comboio das 2 e meia. **d** O senhor e a senhora da Costa vão de férias de barco. **e** Vamos ao cinema no autocarro das 7.15. **f** Viajas de avião? **2 a** compre, **b** comam, **c** partam, **d** viaje, **e** falem, **f** beba. **3** car 1, coach 2, bicycle 3, horse 4, bus 5, on foot 6.

Reading and writing **2** Muitos / públicos / Gosto / metro / caros / o autocarro / uma reunião / vou / de táxi / rápido / a pé / não moro / longe / Às vezes / comboio.

Test yourself **1 a** quer (queres) uma boleia? **b** geralmente viajo de autocarro, **c** queria uma cerveja se faz favor, **d** o comboio é bastante barato, **e** John viaja no autocarro das nove horas, **f** comam o bolo!

2 a Come here! **b** bicycles for hire, **c** health, **d** it's quicker, **e** more than 200 pounds, **f** by coach, **g** outside the city, **h** a large bottle of water, **3 a** quinhentos, **b** setecentos e cinquenta, **c** oito mil, **d** seiscentos e quarenta **e** trezentos e sessenta

Culture round trip

Diálogos 1 **2 a** bus, taxi, boat and train, **b** uma estação de comboios, uma estação de caminho de ferro

Practice 1 **1 a** Há autocarros para Lisboa? **b** A paragem de autocarros é ali à esquerda. **c** O ponto de táxis é ali à direita. **d** A que horas parte o comboio para Faro? **e** Às seis e 15 da tarde. **f** A que horas chega o barco? **g** Há um aeroporto aqui? **h** O terminal é ali, em frente. **i** Para o porto, se faz favor.

Diálogo 2 **2 a** Porto, **b** return, **c** segunda classe

Practice 2 **1 a** Boa tarde, queria dois bilhetes para Loulé, se faz favor. **b** De ida e volta, por favor. **c** Primeira. Qual é a linha para Loulé? **d** A que horas parte o comboio? **e** E a que horas chega? **f** Obrigado/a. **3 Língua viva**: **a** single, **b** 2nd class

Diálogo 3 **2 a** No, because she asks for a list of hotels, **b** hotels, pensions, hostels and a campsite, **c** on the outskirts of town, **d** No, but they have area maps, **e** Here you are.

Diálogos 4 **a** it's on the left, **b** the bank, **c** Go straight on, then take the third street on the left.

Practice 3 **1 a** mercado, **b** estação, **c** Turismo, **2** o mercado / vira / à direita / toma / primeira / à esquerda / segue em frente / à esquina / o mercado / mesmo ali, **3 a** volta, **b** caminho, **c** autocarros, **d** para, **e** classe, **f** horas

Test yourself **1 a** on / to the left, **b** on / to the right, **c** return, **d** Which platform?, **e** Do you have?, **f** on the outskirts, **g** where is?, **h** carry straight on, **i** near / nearby, **j** there outside, **2 a** terminal, **b** a lista, **c** hotel, **d** preço, **e** paragem

Culture to change / exchange, phone card, memory card

Diálogo 1 **2** 100 euros, **3** machine / momento / passport

Practice 1 **1 a** 2, **b** 4, **c** 1, **d** 3, **e** 5, **2 a** for children, **b** no smoking, **c** no parking, **d** open from 10–12, **e** danger, **f** emergency exit, **g** no entry, **h** closed. **3 Língua viva**: **a** Park between 1 and 3 p.m. **b** It's an emergency exit. **c** Primavera shops, **4 1** chamada, **2** passaporte, **3** morada, **4** selos, **5** euros, **6** levantar, **7** cartas, **8** cabine.

Diálogo 3 **2** more or less 80 km

Language discovery Vai demorar um minuto / acho que sim

Practice 2 **1 a** conhece, **b** sabemos, **c** conhecer, **d** conhecem, **e** sabe

Diálogo 3 **2 a** unleaded, **b** fill the tank, **c** air in tyres and 2l of oil, **d** by credit card, **3 a** 4, **b** 8, **c** 1, **d** 9, **e** 10, **f** 5, **g** 7, **h** 2, **i** 6, **j** 3

Diálogo 4 **2 a** from her car, **b** they broke a window, **c** her passport, her purse with money

Test yourself **1 a** certainly / of course, **b** please …, **c** for postcards, **d** in all / in total, **e** toilets / washrooms, **f** roundabout, **g** highway, **h** road signs, **i** in triplicate, **2 a** morada, **b** preencher, **c** queria, **d** uma chamada, **e** dinheiro, **3 a** caminho, **b** seguir, **c** demorar, **d** longe, **e** estrada, **4 a** T, **b** F, **c** F, **d** T, **e** T

UNIT 13

Culture supermercado

Diálogo 1 **2 a** two – oranges and carrots, **b** quantos, **c** they are a bit ripe

Language discovery cauliflower / sardine / lemon / pork / melon / seafood / tomatoes / beef

Language discovery um quilo de batatas / 250 gràmas de mariscos / meio quilo de ameixas / 100 gramas de fígado

Diálogo 2 **2 a** one litre, **b** smoked ham, **c** €5.50

Practice 1 **1** um quilo de cenouras / tres costeletas de porco / 6 fatias de presunto / um pacote de bolachas / duas latas de sopa / uma garrafa de áqua / um tubo de pasta dentífrica / uma dúzia de ovos. **2 Língua viva**: Yes

Listening and reading **2** shoes, sandals, boots, **3 a** no, **b** a blouse, **c** black, **d** high-heeled leather shoes, **4** womenswear: vestido / blusa / saia, menswear: camisa / gravata / jaqueta, shoe section: sapatos / sandálias / botas

Language discovery uma blusa preta

Language discovery sapatos vermelhos / uma gravata verde / uma saia (cor de) rosa

Practice 2 1 a Bom dia. Queria um litro de água e um pão de forma. **b** Não faz mal. Levo um. Tem presunto? **c** Então, pode cortar-me seis fatias, se faz favor. **d** Quero também uma lata de ervilhas e uma barra de sabão. **e** É tudo, obrigado/a. Quanto é?

2

Person	Name of item	Quantity	Price
1	onions	1 kilo	€1.25
2	ham	6 slices	50 cêntimos
3	honey	2 jars	€2.20
4	eggs	10	90 cêntimos
5	sardines	1/2 kilo	€1.70

Test yourself 1 a quilo, **b** é tudo, **c** custa, **d** uma garrafa, **e** em preto, **f** blusa, **g** pescada, **h** uma costeleta, **i** sabão, **j** um par, **2 a** sardinhas, **b** ananás, **c** cabrito, **d** cogumelos, **e** lata, **f** mel

UNIT 14

Culture white wine / red 'green' wine / rosé wine / Port wine

Diálogo 1 2 a milky coffee / espresso / fresh orange juice / mineral water, **b** a menina, **c** pode ser também

Practice 1 1 a uma bica, uma sandes de fiambre, um pastel de nata. **b** um galão, uma sandes de queijo, um pastel de bacalhau, um pastel de nata. **c** um sumo de laranja, uma sandes de fiambre, dois pastéis de bacalhau. **d** um pingado, uma sandes de fiambre, dois pastéis de nata. **e** uma água mineral, um pastel de bacalhau, um pastel de nata.

Diálogo 2 2 a Miguel, **b** He says Miguel must be very hungry, **c** Pepsi, **d** to the cinema, **e** They eat in.

Practice 2 1 answers on the audio, **2 Língua viva**: wine / water

Listening and reading 2 a fish, **b** 365, **c** tripe, **d** pratos típicos, **e** beans

Language discovery meia dose de arroz de mariscos e uma laranja

Tourist menu a pork, **b** soft drink, coffee

Practice 3 1 a Boa noite, tem sopa? **b** Queria um caldo verde. **c** Queria meia dose do bacalhau. Vem com salada? **d** Está bem. **e** Pode ser o pudim

flan. **f** Pode ser meia garrafa de vinho branco e depois, uma bica. **3 (A)**
8,10 **(B)** 1, 12 **(C)** 6,7 **(D)** 3, 9, 14 **(E)** 2, 4, 5 **(F)** 11, 13

Test yourself 1 a milky coffee in a glass, **b** cool, **c** a portion, **d** nothing
else, **e** cabbage (kale) soup, **f** small coffee with milk, **g** fresh orange juice,
h soft drink, **i** draught beer, **j** cover charge, **2 a** porco, **b** frutas, **c** nata,
d fiambre, **e** ananás, **f** limão, **g** verde, **h** chocolate, **i** mariscos, **j** legumes

Culture precisamos dum médico

Language discovery the Portuguese simply say 'hurt the finger, the foot,
the arm' / magoei a mão / ela cortou a perna

Diálogo 1 2 No, but he thinks he's going to.

Practice 1 1 a tenho uma dor de garganta. **b** A minha filha cortou o dedo.
c Doem-me os ouvidos. **d** O meu marido tem insolação. **e** Bati o dedo do
pé. **f** A minha amiga magoou a perna.

2

George Robert Smith
68
10/3/40
Newcastle, Inglaterra.
26 Church Row, Leicester, UK
01634-921550.
(Passport) LL01652B3.
NH5288316.
Mrs J. Green, 43 Market Street
Oxford, UK

Diálogo 2 2 a whether the medicine is for her or a child, and whether she
has other symptoms beyond a sore throat, **b** 2 tablets every 6 hours

Medicines a 4, **b** 1, **c** 3, **d** 5, **e** 2

Practice 2 1 Língua viva: a 7950608. **b** non-emergency calls. **c** National
Help No. (=999). **d** 424124. **e** for the District hospital. **2 a** V, **b** V, **c** F, **d** F, **e** V

Test yourself 1 a centro de saúde, **b** dói-lhe a cabeça, **c** braço, **d** cortei o
dedo, **e** não me sinto bem, **f** precisamos de ajuda, **g** tem alguma coisa
para ...?, **2** posso / não me sinto bem / Dói / garganta / tenho / cortei / o
médico

Culture full-board

Quartos a double bed

Practice 1 **1** full en-suite / 50 euros / it's an extra bed, **3 Língua viva: a** 2 people, **b** it was included

Go further **1** reservar / completa / quarto de casal / extra / 3 anos / individuais / quarto / noites / abril / maio / **a** 2, **b** 9, **c** 6th May, **d** Dear, **2 a** confirmar, **b** ring beforehand, **c** nothing, **d** credit card details

Diálogo 2 **2** the heating isn't working properly

Practice 2 **1 a** 2, **b** 4, **c** 1, **d** 3, **e** 5, **3** answers on the audio **4** answers on the audio

Test yourself **1 a** there are 4 of us, **b** a family room, **c** I'm sorry, **d** thanks for the help, **e** a guest house, **f** with bathroom (en-suite), **g** a twin room, **h** with double bed, **i** the room overlooks the mountains, **j** a form, **2 a** 4, **b** 5, **c** 1, **d** 3, **e** 2

Culture modern art / beach volleyball

Diálogo 1 **2** volleyball, **3** calor / piquenique / sol / contra

Diálogo 2 **2 a** a picnic, **b** lots of things – birds, flowers and so many butterflies, **c** He worked all day.

Language discovery foram ao lago? / fomos

Language discovery (tu) compraste os bolos / (eu) bebi o vinho

Language discovery fui / foram / fomos

Practice 1 **1** (Possible answers) **a** O Paulo foi ao parque. **b** Tu viste o filme. **c** Eu e a Maria visitámos a cidade. **d** Vocês fizeram muitas coisas interessantes. **e** Eu trabalhei ontem. **2 a** Ontem jogámos voleibol. **b** A semana passada visitei o castelo. **c** O ano passado John ficou na floresta. **d** O sábado passado dormiram na praia. **e** Ontem à noite fizeste um bolo. **f** Anteontem a Ana perdeu o telemóvel.

Practice 2 **1 a** 3, **b** 4, **c** 1, **d** 2, **e** 5, **2** answers on the audio

Reading Mother: Activity 2; Father: 5; Sisters: 4; Grandparents: 6

Practice 3 **1 a** fui, **b** visitou, **c** vimos, **d** foram, **e** jogaste, **f** fizeram, **2 a** Strolled in the park with her family and walked through the town centre, **b** a blouse and some sandals, **c** chicken, **d** 7.30 p.m., **e** watched a little television, **3 a** A semana passada eu e a minha irmã visitámos Lisboa. **b** Fomos a um palácio e vimos muitas coisas interessantes. **c** Não, comemos num café na praça. **d** Sim, gostámos muito. **5** Blog: visitou Brasília / comeu / foi à floresta / fez calor / gosto de desportos

Test yourself **1 a** to swim, **b** park, **c** she spoke / has spoken, **d** last week, **e** forest, **f** folklore, **g** picnic, **h** in the shade, **i** I went / I've been, **j** last Monday, **2 a** 3, **b** 7, **c** 1, **d** 8, **e** 5, **f** 6, **g** 2, **h** 4

Portuguese–English vocabulary

a pé *on foot*
aborrecido/a *boring*
abril *April*
aceitar *to accept*
achar *to find, to think*
acidente (o) *accident*
acontecer *to happen, to take place*
Açores (os) *Azores*
adeus *goodbye*
advogado (o) *lawyer*
aeroporto (o) *airport*
África (a) *Africa*
agora *now*
agosto *August*
agradável *pleasant, enjoyable*
água (a) *water*
ajuda (a) *help*
alegre *happy*
além de *as well as*
alface (a) *lettuce*
alguém *someone*
algum/uma *some, any*
ali *over there*
almoçar *to have lunch*
almoço (o) *lunch*
alto/a *tall*
amarelo/a *yellow*
ambiente (o) *atmosphere*
ambulância (a) *ambulance*
ameixa (a) *plum*
América do Sul (a) *South America*
amigo (o) *friend*
ananás (o) *pineapple*
andar *to walk*
andar (o) *floor*
ano (o) *year*

anteontem *the day before yesterday*
antigo/a *old*
anular *to cancel*
ao estrangeiro *abroad*
ao fundo *at the back*
ao lado de *next to*
ao todo *in all, in total*
aos domingos *on Sundays*
aos fins de semana *at weekends*
aos sábados *on Saturdays*
apanhar *to catch*
apanhar o sol *to sunbathe*
apartamento (o) *apartment*
aquecimento (o) *heating*
aquele / aquela *that (m/f)*
aqui *here*
ar (o) *air*
área de beleza natural (a) *area of natural beauty*
areia (a) *sand*
armário (o) *wardrobe, cupboard*
arranjar *to arrange, sort out*
arrogante *arrogant*
arroz de marisco (o) *seafood rice*
arte (a) *art*
artístico/a *artistic*
árvore (a) *tree*
às compras *the shopping*
às vezes *sometimes*
asa (a) *wing*
ascensor (o) *lift*
Ásia (a) *Asia*
aspirina (a) *aspirin*
assado/a *roasted*
assim *so, thus*
assinar *to sign*

assoalhada (a) *room*
até *until, up to*
até à próxima *see you next time*
até breve *see you soon*
até logo, já, amanhã *see you later, soon, tomorrow*
atração (a) *attraction*
atum (o) *tuna*
aula (a) *lesson*
autocarro (o) *bus*
avariado/a *broken down*
avenida (a) *avenue*
avião (o) *aeroplane*
azeite (o) *olive oil*
azul (-claro) *(light-) blue*

bacalhau (o) *salted cod*
baixo/a *short*
banana (a) *banana*
banco (o) *bank*
banqueiro (o) *banker*
barato/a *cheap*
barco (o) *boat*
barra (a) *bar*
barulhento/a *noisy*
barulho (o) *noise*
bastante *quite*
batata (a) *potato*
bater *to bang*
bem *well*
biblioteca (a) *library*
bica (a) *espresso coffee*
bicicleta (a) *bicycle*
bilhete (o) *ticket*
bilhete de (ida e) volta (o) *return, round-trip ticket*
bilhete simples / de ida (o) *single / one-way ticket*
blusa (a) *blouse*
boa noite *good evening / night, hello (or goodbye)*
boa tarde *good afternoon / evening, hello*

boa! *good idea!*
boca (a) *mouth*
bolacha (a) *biscuit*
boleia (a) *lift (in a vehicle)*
bolo (o) *cake*
bom dia *good morning, hello*
bombeiros (os) *firefighters*
bonito/a *pretty*
borboleta (a) *butterfly*
bota (a) *boot*
braço (o) *arm*
branco/a *white*
Brasil (o) *Brazil*
brasileiro/a *Brazilian*
Brigada do Trânsito (a) *traffic police*

cá *here*
cabeça (a) *head*
cabedal (o) *leather*
cabine telefónica(a) *phone booth*
cabrito (o) *kid (goat)*
cada *every*
café (o) *cafe, coffee*
café-bar (o) *cafe-bar*
caixa (a) *cash desk, till, box*
calças (as) *trousers*
caldo verde (o) *kale soup*
calmo/a *calm*
calor (o) *heat*
cama (a) *bed*
cambiar *to change*
câmbio (o) *currency exchange*
caminho (o) *way, road*
camioneta (a) *coach*
camisa (a) *shirt*
campo (o) *countryside*
caneca (a) *pint (beer)*
carapau (o) *mackerel*
carne (a) *meat*
carne de porco (a) *pork*
caro/a *expensive*
carregador (o) *charger*
carro (o) *car*

carta (a) *letter*
cartão (o) bancário *bank card*
   telefónico *phone card*
   de crédito *credit card*
cartão (o) de memória *memory card*
   europeu de saúde *European Health Card (EHIC)*
carteira (a) *wallet, purse*
casa (a) *house*
casa de banho (a) *bathroom*
casa de modas (a) *fashion house*
casa de pasto (a) *cheap eating place*
casal (o) *couple, double*
casinha (a) *cottage, small house*
castelo (o) *castle*
catedral (a) *cathedral*
cavalo (o) *horse*
cebola (a) *onion*
cedo *early*
celebração (a) *celebration*
cenoura (a) *carrot*
cêntimo (o) *cent*
central (a) rodoviária / de camionagem *bus / coach station*
centro (o) *centre*
centro comercial (o) *shopping centre*
centro de saúde (o) *health centre*
certo/a *correct*
cerveja (a) *beer*
céu (o) *sky*
chamada (a) *phone call*
chamar-se *to be called*
charmoso/a *charming*
chefe (o) *boss*
chegar *to arrive*
cheio/a de *full of*
chover *to rain*
chuva (a) *rain*
chuveiro (o) *shower (in bathroom)*
cidade (a) *town, city*
claro *of course*
clássico/a *classic*
coisa (a) *thing*

coitado/a, coitadinho/a *poor thing, poor little thing*
coleção (a) *collection*
com *with*
com certeza *certainly, of course*
com licença *excuse me*
comboio (o) *train*
começar *to begin*
comer *to eat*
comida (a) *food*
como *how*
como é? *what is it like?*
como está? *how are you?*
completamente *completely*
comprar *to buy*
compras (as) *shopping*
comprimido (o) *pill*
comunicar *to report*
concerto (o) *concert*
conduzir *to drive*
conhecer *to (get to) know, be acquainted with*
conjunto (o) *ladies' suit*
connosco *with us*
constipado/a *with a bad cold*
consulta (a) *consultation*
conter *to contain*
continuar *to continue*
contra *against*
convento (o) *convent*
cor (a) *colour*
correio (o) *post office*
correr *to run*
corrigir *to correct*
cortar *to cut*
corte de eletricidade (o) *power cut*
costas (as) *back (body)*
costeleta (a) *chop (meat)*
costurar *to sew*
coxa (a) *chicken drumstick, thigh*
cozinha (a) *cuisine, kitchen*
crer *to believe, think*
criança (a) *child*

cuidado! *careful!*
cultura (a) *culture*
cultural *cultural*
custar *to cost*

daqui *from here*
dar *to give*
de *from, of, by (transport)*
de ... em ... (horas) *every ... (hours)*
de ida e volta *return*
de nada *don't mention it*
de onde é / são? *where are you from?*
   (sing / pl)
de vez em quando *sometimes*
debaixo de *underneath*
dedo (do pé) (o) *finger (toe)*
deitar-se *to lie down, to go to bed*
deixar *to leave*
delicioso/a *delicious*
demorar *to take (time)*
dentista (o/a) *dentist*
depois *then, after*
depósito (o) *petrol tank*
desagradável *unpleasant*
desculpa/e! *excuse me!*
desempregado/a *unemployed*
desportivo/a *sporty*
desportos (os) *sports*
desportos aquáticos (os) *aquatic*
   sports
detrás de *behind*
dezembro *December*
dia de anos (o) *birthday*
difícil *difficult*
diga lá! *tell me, say, come on!*
Dinamarca (a) *Denmark*
dinamarquês/esa *Danish*
dinheiro (o) *money*
direita; à _____ *right; on the _____*
dizer *to say*
doente *sick, unwell*
doer *to hurt, have pain*
domingo *Sunday*

dona de casa (a) *housewife*
dormir *to sleep*
dose (a) *portion*
duplo/a *double, twin (room)*
durante *during*
dúzia (a) *dozen*

e *and*
é *is, you are (sing.)*
edifício (o) *building*
elegante *elegant*
elevador (o) *lift*
em *in, on*
em baixo *downstairs, below*
em casa *at home*
em cima *upstairs, above*
em cima de *on top of*
em família *as a family*
em frente de *in front of*
em geral *generally*
empresa (a) *business, company*
encher *to fill*
enfermeiro/a *nurse*
engraçado/a *funny*
então *well then*
entre *in between*
entrecosto (o) *entrecôte*
enxaqueca (a) *migraine*
ervilha (a) *pea*
escalope (o) *slice (scallop)*
escola (a) *school*
escola secundária (a) *secondary*
   school
escolher *to choose*
escritor/a *writer*
escritório (o) *office*
espadarte (o) *sword fish*
Espanha (a) *Spain*
espanhol/ola *Spanish*
espetáculo (o) *show, event*
esporte (o) *sport (Brazilian)*
esquadra da polícia (a) *police station*
esquerda; à _____ *left; on the _____*

esquina (a) *corner*
está boa? *are you well? (to a lady)*
estação (a) *station*
estação (a) de comboios *train station*
 comboios / *station*
 de caminho de ferro C.F. *railway*
 station
estacionado/a *parked*
estalagem (a) *inn*
estante (a) *bookcase*
estar *to be*
estás bom? *are you well? (to a man,*
 informal)
este / esta *this (m / f)*
estilo (o) *style*
estômago (o) *stomach*
estou bem *I'm well*
estou ótimo/a *I'm fine*
estrada (a) *highway*
estrangeiro/a *foreigner*
estrela (a) *star*
estudante (o/a) *student*
eu *I*
euro (o) *euro*
Europa (a) *Europe*
evento (musical) (o) *(musical) event*
exatamente *exactly*
exótico/a *exotic*
experimentar *to try (on)*

fácil *easy*
falar *to speak*
falo *I speak*
família (a) *family*
farmacêutico (o) *pharmacist*
farmácia (a) *pharmacy*
fatia (a) *thin slice*
faz / faça favor de ... *please ...*
fazer *to do, make*
fazer surf, anos, calor *to surf, to have a*
 birthday, be hot
feijoada (a) *bean stew*
feijões (os) *beans*
feira (a) *fair, market*

férias (as) *holidays*
festa (de anos) (a) *(birthday) party*
fevereiro *February*
fiambre (o) *ham*
fica *is situated*
ficar *to stay, be (situated), become*
ficar com *to keep*
ficha (a) *form*
fígado (o) *liver*
filha (a) *daughter*
filho (o) *son*
filhos (os) *children, sons*
fino (o) *small draft beer (north of*
 Portugal)
flores (as) *flowers*
floresta (a) *forest*
fogão (o) *cooker*
folheto (o) *leaflet*
fome (a) *hunger*
fora (de) *outside*
fora da cidade *outside the city*
formulário (o) *form*
forno (o) *oven*
fósforos (os) *matches*
França (a) *France*
frango (o) *chicken*
frasco (o) *jar*
freguês/esa (o/a) *customer*
fresco/a *cooled, ice-cold*
frigorífico (o) *fridge*
frio/a *cold*
funcionar *to work*
furo (o) *puncture*
futebol (o) *football*

galão (o) *milky coffee*
galeria (de arte) (a) *(art) gallery*
garagem (a) *garage*
garrafa (a) *bottle*
garrafão (o) *large bottle*
gasóleo (o) *diesel*
gasolina (a) *petrol*
gato (o) *cat*
gelado (o) *ice cream*

geleia (a) jam
gente (a) people
geralmente generally
golfe (o) golf
gosta/am? do you like? (sing / pl)
gostamos we like
gostar to like
gostaria de I would like to
grama (o) gram
grande big
gravata (a) tie
Grécia (a) Greece
grego/a Greek
gripe (a) flu
Guarda Nacional Republicana (GNR)
    (a) National Guard

há there is / are
há meia hora half an hour ago
haver to have, be
havia there was, were
hipermercado (o) hypermarket
histórico/a historical
hoje today
Holanda (a) Holland
homem (o) man
honesto/a honest
horário (o) timetable
hospital (o) hospital
hotel (o) hotel
houve there was, has been

ida (a) single (ticket)
ida e volta (a) return (ticket)
idade (a) age
ideal ideal
igreja (a) church
igualmente likewise
ilha (a) island
ilha da Madeira (a) Madeira island
imenso a lot
imperial (a) small draft beer
incluído/a included

incluindo including
individual single (room)
informação/ões (a, as) information
inglês/esa English
insolação (o) sunstroke
instantinho (o) moment
inteiro/a whole
interessante interesting
introduzir to insert
inverno (o) winter
ir to go
irmã (a) sister
irmão (o) brother
isolado/a isolated

já está there it is, that's it
janeiro January
jantar to dine
jantar (o) dinner
Japão (o) Japan
jaqueta (a) jacket
jardim (o) garden
javali (o) wild boar
jogar to play (sport)
jogar cartas to play cards
jogo, jogão (o) game, big game
jornais (os) newspapers
jovem young
julho July
junho June

lá fora out there
lá, ali there
lago (o) lake
lama (a) mud
lamentar to be sorry
laranja (cor de) orange colour
laranjas (as) oranges
lareira (a) fireplace
lata (a) tin, can
lavabos (os) washroom and toilet
leio I read
leitão (o) suckling pig

leite (o) *milk*
ler *to read*
levantar dinheiro *to withdraw money*
levantar-se *to get up*
levar *to take, to take out*
libras (as) *pounds*
limpar *to clean*
limpo/a *clean*
linha (a) *platform*
lista (a) *list, menu*
litoral (o) *coast*
litro (o) *litre*
livrinho (o) *small book*
livro (o) *book*
logo *soon, then*
loja (a) *shop*
Londres *London*
longe *a long way*
lugar (o) *place*
lulas (as) *squid*

maçã (a) *apple*
maçada (a) *pain, drag*
maduro/a *ripe*
mãe (a) *mother*
magoar *to hurt*
maio *May*
maior *bigger*
mais de *more than*
mais ou menos *more or less*
mais tarde *later*
mala (a) *bag*
mandar *to send*
manteiga (a) *butter*
mapa (o) *map*
máquina (a) *machine*
máquina de lavar (a) *washing machine*
máquina fotográfica (a) *camera*
mar (o) *sea*
maravilhoso/a *wonderful*
março *March*
marido (o) *husband*

mariscos (os) *seafood*
mas *but*
médico/a (o) *doctor*
meia-pensão (a) *half board*
meio quilo (o) *half a kilo*
mel (o) *honey*
melancia (a) *watermelon*
melhor *better*
melhorar *to improve*
mercado (o) *market*
mercearia (a) *grocer's*
mergulhar *to dive*
mês (o) *month*
mesa (a) *table*
mesmo ali *right there*
metro(politano) (o) *metro / underground*
minimercado (o) *minimart*
moderno/a *modern*
molhado/a *wet*
monumento (o) *monument*
morada (a) *address*
morango (o) *strawberry*
morar *to live*
mosteiro (o) *monastery*
moto(cicleta) (a) *motorbike*
movimentado/a *busy*
muitas vezes *often*
muito *very, a lot, much*
muito bem *very well*
muito prazer *pleased to meet you*
mulher (a) *wife, woman*
multibanco (o) *ATM cash machine*
mundo (o) *world*
museu (o) *museum*
música (a) *music*

na *in / on the*
na moda *in fashion*
nacional *national*
nada *nothing*
nadar *to swim*
namorado/a (o/a) *boy/girlfriend*

não *no, not*
não faz mal *don't worry, no problem*
não funciona *it doesn't work*
nariz (o) *nose*
natureza (a) *nature*
navegar na internet *to surf the net*
nervoso/a *nervous*
nevar *to snow*
neve (a) *snow*
no ano que vem *next year*
no/na *in, on the*
nome (o) *name*
nos arredores *on the outskirts*
novembro *November*
novo/a *young, new*
número (o) *number*
nunca *never*

o que (é que)? *what (is it that)?*
o que faz? *what do you do?*
objetos (os) *objects*
obrigadinho/a *thanks*
obrigado/a *thank you*
oferecer *to offer*
olá *hi*
óleo (o) *oil*
olho (o) *eye*
onde *where*
ônibus (o) *bus (Brazilian)*
ontem *yesterday*
ontem à noite *last night*
ópera (a) *opera*
oportunidade (a) *opportunity*
ora bem! *well now! / right then!*
organizar *to organize*
orgulhoso/a *proud*
ou *or*
ou ... ou ... *either ... or ...*
outono (o) *autumn*
outros (os) *(the) others*
outubro *October*

ouvir *to listen to*
ovos (os) *eggs*

pacote (o) *packet*
padrão (o) *style*
pai (o) *father*
país (o) *country*
pais (os) *parents*
palácio (o) *palace*
pão (o) *bread*
pãozinho (o) *bread roll*
papel (higiénico) (o) *(toilet) paper*
par (o) *pair*
para *in order to*
para nós / mim / si *for us / me / you (him, her)*
para o ano *next year*
parabéns! *congratulations!*
paragem (a) *(bus) stop*
parede (a) *wall*
parque (o) *park*
parque (o) de campismo *camping park*
partido/a *broken*
partir *to depart, break*
passado/a *past, last*
passaporte (o) *passport*
passar *to pass*
passar tempo *to spend time*
pássaro (o) *bird*
passear *to stroll*
pasta dentífrica (a) *toothpaste*
pastel de bacalhau (o) *fishcake*
pastel de nata (o) *custard pastry tart*
pastelaria (a) *cake shop*
pé (o) *foot*
pechincha (a) *bargain*
pedir *to ask for, order*
pedir desculpa *to be sorry*
peito (o) *chest*
pelo menos *at least*

pensão (a) *guest house*
pensão-completa (a) *full-board*
pequeno/a *small*
pequeno-almoço (o) *breakfast*
pêras (as) *pears*
perdão *pardon*
pergunta (a) *question*
perigoso/a *dangerous*
perna (a) *leg*
perto (daqui) *near (here)*
peru (o) *turkey*
pescada (a) *hake*
pescar *to fish*
pessoalmente *personally*
pimentão (o) *(green) pepper*
pintar *to paint*
piquenique (o) *picnic*
piscina (a) *swimming pool*
planta (a) *town plan*
poder *to be able*
pode-se *you (one) can*
pois *well, er, erm*
poltrona (a) *armchair*
por *by, along, through*
pôr *to put*
por causa de *because of, on account of*
por favor *please*
por noite *per night*
porque *because*
porta (a) *door*
portagem (a) *toll*
portanto *therefore*
porto (o) *port*
Portugal Continental *mainland Portugal*
português/esa *Portuguese*
posso? *may I?*
postal (o) *postcard*
pote (o) *pot, jar*
poucas vezes *few times, seldom*
pouquinho (um) *a little bit*

pousada (a) *high-class hotel*
pousada de juventude (a) *youth hostel*
praça (a) *square*
praça de táxis (a) *taxi rank*
praia (a) *beach*
precisar de *to need*
preço (o) *price*
prédio (o) *building*
preencher *to fill in*
preferido/a *preferred, favourite*
preferir *to prefer*
preguiçoso/a *lazy*
presunto (o) *smoked ham*
preto/a *black*
primavera (a) *spring*
primeiro/a *first*
problema (o) *problem*
professor/ora *teacher*
programa (o) *programme*
próprio/a *own*
proteção (a) *protection*
provar *to try, taste*
provavelmente *probably*
próximo *nearby*
pudim flan (o) *crème caramel*

quadro (o) *picture*
qual? *which?*
qualidade (a) *quality*
qualquer coisa *something*
quanto é? *how much is it?*
quanto? *how much?*
quantos/as? *how many?*
quarta-feira (a) *Wednesday*
quarto (o) *a 25 cl bottle*
quarto (o) *bedroom*
quarto de casal / para família (o) *double room / room for a family*
que *that, which*
que mais? *what else?*

que tal? *how about it?*
queijo (o) *cheese*
quem? *who?*
quente *hot*
querer *to want, to wish*
quilo (o) *kilo*
quilómetro (o) *kilometre*
quinhentos *500*
quinta-feira (a) *Thursday*
quinze dias *fortnight*
quotidiano/a *everyday*

rancho folclórico (o) *folklore group*
rápido (direto) (o) *express (direct) train*
rápido/a *fast*
receção (a) *reception*
recomendar *to recommend*
rede social (a) *social network*
refeição/ões (a, as) *meal(s)*
reformado/a *retired*
refrigerante (o) *soft drink*
região (a) *region*
relaxante *relaxing*
remédio (o) *medicine*
renda (a) *lacemaking*
repolho (o) *cabbage*
rés-do-chão (o) *ground floor*
reservado/a *reserved*
reservar *to reserve*
residencial (a) *guest house*
restaurante (o) *restaurant*
resto (o) do dia *the rest of the day*
retrete (a) *separate toilet*
reunião (a) *meeting*
revista (a) *magazine*
risco (o) *risk*
rolo (o) *roll*
romântico/a *romantic*
rosa (cor de) *rose (colour)*
rotina diária (a) *daily routine*
rotunda (a) *roundabout*
roubo (o) *theft*
roupas (as) *clothes*
rua (a) *road*

sábado (o) *Saturday*
sabão (o) *soap*
saber *to know a fact, how to do something*
saia (a) *skirt*
saída (a) *exit*
sair *to go out*
sal (o) *salt*
sala (a) *living room, lounge*
sala de estar (a) *living room, lounge*
sala de jantar (a) *dining room*
salto alto (de) *high heeled*
sandálias (as) *sandals*
sandes (a) *sandwich*
sanita (a) *toilet bowl*
sanitários (os) *public toilets*
sapataria (a) *shoe shop*
sapatos (os) *shoes*
sardinhas (as) *sardines*
saudades (as) *nostalgia, longing*
saudável *healthy*
saúde (a) *health*
se *if*
se calhar *probably*
seguir *to follow*
segunda-feira (a) *Monday*
segundo/a *second*
selo (o) *stamp*
sem *without*
sem chumbo *unleaded*
semana (passada) (a) *(last) week*
sempre *always*
senhor (o) / senhora (a) *sir / madam, you (polite)*
senhores (os) *you (pl. polite)*
sentar-se *to sit down*
sentir-se *to feel*
ser *to be*
sério/a *serious*
serra (a) *mountain range*
setembro *September*
sexta-feira (a) *Friday*
sim *yes*
simpático/a *nice*

simples *single (ticket, room)*
sinais (os) *road signs*
sintoma (o) *symptom*
só *only, just*
sobremesa (a) *dessert*
sofá (o) *sofa*
sol (o) *sun*
solitário/a *lonely*
sombra (a) *shade*
sossego (o) *quiet*
sotaque (o) *accent*
sou de *I am from*
sozinho/a *alone*
Suíça (a) *Switzerland*
sujo/a *dirty*
sumo (o) *fruit juice*
supermercado (o) *supermarket*

talvez haja *perhaps there is, there may be*
tamanho (o) *size*
também *also*
tantos/as *so many*
tarde (a) *afternoon*
tasca (a) *cheap eating place*
táxi (o) *taxi*
tchau! *bye!*
teatro (o) *theatre*
telemóvel (o) *mobile phone*
telenovelas (as) *soap operas*
televisão (a) *television*
tempo de lazer (o) *leisure time*
tempo livre (o) *free time*
tenda (a) *tent*
ténis (o) *tennis*
tentar *to try*
ter *to have*
terça-feira (a) *Tuesday*
terceiro/a *third*
terminal (o) *bus terminus*
terra (a) *land, hometown*
terraço (o) *balcony*
testemunha (a) *witness*
tímido/a *shy*

tinto *red (wine)*
tipicamente *typically*
típico/a *typical*
tirar férias *to take/have a holiday*
todas as noites *every night*
todos os anos (os) *every year*
todos os dias *every day*
tomar *to take (food, drink, medicine)*
tomar banho *to have a bath (shower, wash)*
tomaste ...? *have you taken ...?*
tonto/a *dizzy*
trabalhador/a *hard-working*
trabalhar *to work*
trabalho (o) *work*
transeunte (o) *passer-by*
transporte público (o) *public transport*
trem (o) *train (Brazilian)*
tripas (as) *tripe*
triplicado/a *triplicate*
trocar *to change*
tu *you (familiar)*
tudo *everything, all*
turismo (o) *tourism, tourist office*
turismo (o) rural/ de habitação *rural tourism/ homestay tourism*

um momento *one moment*
um pouco *a bit, little*
um pouco de ... *a bit of ...*
uma vez por ... *once a ...*
único/a *only*
universidade(a) *university*

vago/a *free, available*
vários/as *various*
vaso (o) *vase*
vela (a) *candle*
velho/a *old*
vender *to sell*
vende-se *for sale*
vento (o) *wind*
ver *to see, to watch*
verão (o) *summer*

verde (-escuro) *(dark) green*
vermelho/a *red*
vestido (o) *dress*
vestir-se *to get dressed*
vez (a) *time (occasion)*
viagem (a) *journey*
viajar *to travel*
vida (a) *life*
videojogo (o) *videogame*
vidro (o) *window, glass*
vinho (o) *wine*

vir *to come*
vista (a) *view*
vista de olhos (a) *glance, look*
viver *to live*
você *you*
voleibol (o) *volleyball*
voltar *to turn, to return*
vomitar *to be sick, to throw up*

xarope (o) *syrup, cough remedy*

Numbers

um (uma)	1	vinte e um (uma)	21
dois (duas)	2	trinta	30
três	3	quarenta	40
quatro	4	cinquenta	50
cinco	5	sessenta	60
seis	6	setenta	70
sete	7	oitenta	80
oito	8	noventa	90
nove	9	cem (cento)	100
dez	10	cento e um (uma)	101
onze	11	duzentos/as	200
doze	12	trezentos/as	300
treze	13	quatrocentos/as	400
catorze	14	quinhentos/as	500
quinze	15	seiscentos/as	600
dezasseis	16	setecentos/as	700
dezassete	17	oitocentos/as	800
dezoito	18	novecentos/as	900
dezanove	19	mil	1,000
vinte	20	un milhão	1,000,000

primeiro/a, 1º/1ª	first	sexto/a, 6º/6ª	sixth
segundo/a, 2º/2ª	second	sétimo/a, 7º/7ª	seventh
terceiro/a, 3º/3ª	third	oitavo/a, 8º/8ª	eighth
quarto/a, 4º/4ª	fourth	nono/a, 9º/9ª	ninth
quinto/a, 5º/5ª	fifth	décimo/a, 10º/10ª	tenth